THE

TRUTH

WILL SET

YOU

FREE

THE
TRUTH
WILL SET
YOU
FREE

*Overcoming Emotional Blindness
and Finding Your True
Adult Self*

BASIC
BOOKS

A MEMBER OF THE PERSEUS BOOKS GROUP

CONTENTS

Part I

CHILDHOOD: THE UNTAPPED SOURCE OF KNOWLEDGE

Part II

HOW WE ARE STRUCK
EMOTIONALLY BLIND

Part III

BREAKING THROUGH: DISCOVERING OUR
CHILDHOOD HISTORIES

PREFACE

———————————

*I*WROTE THIS book not for professionals but for readers who want to think about their lives and test new ideas—hence the absence of psychological jargon. Three terms that I have elaborated in my earlier work figure largely here, however, and they require a word of explanation for readers coming to my work for the first time.

Poisonous pedagogy is a phrase I use to refer to the kind of parenting and education aimed at breaking a child's will and making that child into an obedient subject by means of overt or covert coercion, manipulation, and emotional blackmail.

In my books *For Your Own Good* and *Thou Shalt Not Be Aware*, I have explained the concept using concrete examples. In my other books I have repeatedly stressed how the mendacious mentality behind this approach to dealing with children can leave long-lasting imprints on the way we think and relate to one another in our adult lives.

A *helping witness* is a person who stands by an abused child (consistently or occasionally), offering support and acting as a balance against the cruelty otherwise dominant in the child's everyday life. This can be anyone from the child's immediate world: a teacher, a neighbor, a caregiver, a grandmother, often a sibling.

Helping witnesses give sympathy and affection to these beaten or neglected children. They trust the children and help them feel that they are not bad or evil but worthy of kindness from others. Thanks to such witnesses, who may be completely oblivious to the role they are playing, children in difficult situations can see that there is such a thing as love in this world. In the best cases they learn how to develop trust in their fellow humans and to accept the love and kindness that come their way.

In the total absence of helping witnesses these children glorify the violence they have been subjected to and frequently make blatant use of it in later life. (It is no coincidence that as children, mass murderers like Hitler, Stalin, and Mao had no helping witnesses to turn to.)

In adult life, a role similar to that of childhood's helping witness may be taken over by an *enlightened witness*. By this I mean someone who is aware of the consequences that neglect and cruelty in childhood can have. Enlightened witnesses support these harmed individuals, empathize with them, and help them gain an understanding of their feelings of anxiety and powerlessness as products of their own history rather than as some frightening, mysterious force. This knowledge makes it easier to appreciate the options open to them as adults.

Therapists can qualify as enlightened witnesses, as can well-informed and open-minded teachers, lawyers, counselors, and writers. I see myself as an author whose books are, among other things, designed to convey information that is still frequently considered taboo. My goal is also to help experts—therapists, counselors, educators—understand their own lives better and thus become enlightened witnesses for their clients, patients, children, and, not least, for themselves. Sometimes I have been successful in this endeavor, as is shown by the following excerpt from a letter written to me by a European poet and singer:

Dear Alice Miller,

I am writing to you and sending the enclosed CD as a way of thanking you for the support and help you have given me for so many years. I have had my songs translated into German so that you can read them in your own language.

I remember very well that whenever the present consequences of my past were at their most tormenting, your books were my link with reality. The things I found out about my childhood from the lyrics of my own songs came as a shock. What they revealed was appalling. For a long time I closed my eyes to what I knew deep down and the consequences that were bound to follow if I accepted it. My whole body was crying out and I did not understand why. But with those words, carried by the music and intuitively slipping past the censor on guard within, I came close to what I was trying to tell myself. Slowly, experiences I never knew I had started unfolding before me. If at this sensitive stage I had not had the good fortune to encounter your books, telling me so clearly that I was not alone, I do not know how long I might have gone on suppressing what my inner self was trying to get through to me.

Finally the support from your books gave me the courage to seek help from a psychotherapist, and the sessions with him were the next stage in my labor of self-discovery. At last I was able to share my suppressed experiences with someone and gradually uncover what I had always felt I must hide from myself. Confronting the people who had exposed me to such interference with my self confirmed that my emotional memory had told me the truth. Then it was easier to find a remedy. But I was lucky all the same. With a bad therapist I would have been thrown off the track and lost a lot of time. The way back is long enough as it is, and shortcuts are often deceptive.

Without the information your books communicated to me I would not have been properly able to accept what I read in my sons' eyes about my self. With my lack of freedom and my early isolation, I would have stood in the way of their freedom even more than I did. I am happy to have found help and support in my attempt to find my way back to the path of my life. When numbing guilt from my past surfaces and tells me I have no right to live, I frequently reach for one of your books and read for a while. That gives me the courage to go on.

In *The Drama of the Gifted Child* I described the suffering of children forced to live in a world in which their feelings are ignored and denied. My stories helped many readers discover their own personal histories, which they had kept hidden from themselves. In my later books I demonstrated that this denial and repression of childhood suffering, and the blindness to it in later life that I identified in my clients, hold true for many others. In the works of major writers, philosophers, and artists—including Kafka, Flaubert, Beckett, Picasso, Soutine, van Gogh, and Nietzsche—I was able to show the traces their childhoods had left on them and was amazed at the similarities among their life stories. In the childhoods of the worst tyrants in history I discovered a recurring pattern: extreme cruelty, idealization of the parents, glorification of violence, denial of pain, and revenge wreaked on whole nations and peoples as a way of getting even for the cruelty they had once experienced and then denied.

Today the problem of child abuse looms large in our public awareness. What is less well known is that what we consider a proper upbringing frequently includes severe humiliations that have far-reaching consequences—humiliations we do not consciously recognize because we have been rendered incapable of perceiving them at the very beginning of our lives. The result is a vicious circle of violence and ignorance.

How does this vicious circle work?

1. The traditional methods of upbringing, which have included corporal punishment, lead a child to deny suffering and humiliation.

2. This denial, although essential if the child is to survive, will later cause emotional blindness, especially parental emotional blindness.

3. Emotional blindness produces "barriers in the mind" erected to guard against dangers. This means that early denied traumas become encoded in the brain, and even though they no longer pose a threat, they continue to be an insidious hazard.

4. Barriers in the mind stunt our capacity to learn from new information, to put it to good use, and to shed old, outdated programs.

5. Our bodies retain a complete memory of the humiliations we suffered, driving us to inflict unconsciously on the next generation what we endured in childhood.

6. Barriers in the mind make it difficult, if not impossible, to avoid this repetition, unless we firmly resolve to identify the cause of our behavior as deeply embedded in the history of our own childhoods. But this rarely happens. Far too many of us simply replay what our parents and our parents' parents and their parents before them have done, stubbornly and blindly repeating: Spare the rod, spoil the child.

The philosopher Karl Popper once wrote that an assertion can claim to be scientific only if it is capable of being falsified. I have abided by that definition, and in this book I again state my claims in a way that can be verified or disproved. You are free to check the veracity of my assertions against your own experiences, as many readers of my other books have done.

But the main purpose of my book is to stimulate reflection—reflection on our own lives and those important stories and histories hidden away in our families. I hope it helps enhance your understanding of what goes on around you and in yourself.

In the first section of the book, "Childhood: The Untapped Source of Knowledge," I discuss the ways in which the subject of childhood is consistently evaded, even when one would expect the opposite to be the case.

The second section, "How We Are Struck Emotionally Blind," draws on the latest brain research to explain *why* evading childhood reality is so widespread.

In Part III, "Breaking Through: Discovering Our Childhood Histories," I present several people who have succeeded in retrieving their childhood realities and, reaping the benefits of that accomplishment, have rid themselves of their parental emotional blindness.

In the Epilogue I plead for an end to emotional blindness and to the story of the forbidden fruit. In the age of the Internet we have access to almost unlimited information. Nobody can forbid us to find our truth and to understand the crucial difference between good and evil, between being free to love or being trapped by the compulsion to inflict our old suffering on others.

THOU
SHALT NOT
KNOW

WHEN I WAS a child, the story of Creation was for me above all the story of the forbidden fruit. I could not understand why Adam and Eve should not be allowed to have knowledge. To me, knowledge and awareness were wonderful things. So I failed to see the logic behind God's decision to forbid Adam and Eve to recognize the essential difference between good and evil.

My childhood stubbornness on this point lost none of its vigor when I later encountered other interpretations of the story of Creation. At an emotional level I simply refused to see obedience as a virtue, curiosity as a sin, and ignorance of good and evil as an ideal state. To my way of thinking, the apple from the tree of knowledge promised an explanation of evil and hence represented redemption—good as opposed to evil.

There are countless theological explanations for the motives behind God's inscrutable counsels, but in all too many of them I see a terrorized child trying hard to interpret the mysterious actions of the parents as good and loving, even though the child cannot fathom them—indeed, has no chance of fathoming them. The motives behind them are unfathomable even for the parents themselves, hidden away as they are in the dark recesses of their own childhood.

I have never understood why God would tolerate the presence of Adam and Eve in the Garden of Eden only if they remained ignorant and why they were punished so severely for their disobedience. I never felt any yearnings for a paradise where obedience and ignorance are the conditions for beatitude. I believe in the power of love, but for me love is not synonymous with being "good" in the sense of being obedient. Love has something to do with being true to oneself and one's feelings and needs. And the desire for knowledge is part of that. God obviously set out to deprive Adam and Eve of this loyalty to themselves. But why? My conviction is that we can love only if we are allowed to be what we are: no pretense, no disguises, no facades. We can genuinely love only if we do *not* deny ourselves the knowledge available to us (like the tree of knowledge in the Garden), if, instead of fleeing from it, we have the simple courage to eat the apple.

I still find it difficult to summon up any kind of tolerance when I hear it said that children have to be beaten to make them "good" and to ensure that God will take pleasure in them. The story of Creation has long prevented us from opening our eyes and recognizing that we have been misguided.

The following examples illustrate the high price, in terms of health, we pay for the ban on knowledge. I recently received a letter from a stranger who has been a member of the Communist party for decades. He was also on the editorial board of a newspaper disseminating the ideas of many Marxist philosophers. Chancing upon my work a number of years back, he attempted to engage in an exchange with his colleagues about the view that violence and the desire for power are learned in childhood, and that the subject of education by the use of force should be integrated into Marxist thinking. Despite the virulent animosity he encountered, he became more and more convinced that he was on the right path. During this period he suffered from severe arthritis in his feet, making it impossible for him to walk. When he finally resolved to notify the Communist party in writing that he had decided to leave it, he was assailed by massive anxieties bound up with the abandonment he had suffered as a child of a religious family with strict Protestant rules of discipline, a child who never had the right to his own opinions without the threat of punishment and emotional abandonment.

To his surprise and joy, three hours after giving his "no-tice," the pain in his feet disappeared. He saw this as proof that he had succeeded in refusing to perpetuate the situation he had been in as a child and in breaking out of a state of dependency that, though affording him the illusion of security in the past, had started to stifle him. The man was astounded at the speed of the bodily response to his action. He knew, though, that this was not a case of "miracle heal-ing" in the usual sense of the term but the logical conse-quence of his decision to walk out of the prison in which he had been incarcerated.

Although scientific medicine no longer denies that our bodies store information about what we have experienced in our lives, it is frequently at a loss to decipher those ex-periences. Yet we know of instances in which severe phys-ical symptoms vanish when one succeeds in surmounting such experiences.

Here is another example. A man who had been severely humiliated and abused in his childhood idealized his par-ents all his life. In old age, when his immune system was compromised, he came down with a serious physical ail-ment. The messages from his cognitive system told him that everything in his childhood was good and that he had been lucky to have such ideal parents to care for him. But his physical symptom was signaling precisely the opposite, the story the man had spent all his life preferring to ignore. For years he took medications and underwent operations until finally, on the advice of an internist, he began seeing a psychotherapist.

From then on, there was no concealing the terror that this man had been exposed to as a child. He had spent sixty years denying it before finding the courage to face up to the truth. When he regained his health it seemed like a miracle, but there was nothing miraculous about it. If your cognitive system asserts the opposite of what the cells in your body unerringly identify as the truth, you will be living in a state of permanent inner discord. But once both systems are allowed to have the same knowledge, the bodily functions can resume their normal activity.

I can remember as a child causing my parents embarrassment by asking questions they found difficult to answer. I bit back the questions that were on the tip of my tongue. But they come back again and again, and I intend to make use of my freedom as an adult to let the child within finally ask the questions she always wanted to ask.

Why did God plant the tree of knowledge right in the middle of the Garden of Eden if He didn't want the two people He had created to eat the fruit? Why did He, the almighty God who created Heaven and Earth, lead His creatures into temptation and force them into obedience? If He was omniscient, He must have known that in creating humans He had made beings who would be curious by nature, and that He would be forcing them to be untrue to their nature. Why might He have done that? And what

would have happened if Eve had not partaken of the fruit?
There would have been no sexual union, so Adam and Eve
would never have had any children. Would the world have
stayed barren and empty? Would Adam and Eve have lived
forever, alone, without children?

Why is having children bound up with sin? Why is the
act of giving birth so painful? How are we to understand
that God planned these two human creatures to be infer-
tile, although the story of Creation talks of how the birds
and the beasts are actively enjoined to go forth and multi-
ply? God must have had a concept of reproduction. Later
we are told that Cain married and had children. But if
there was no one else on earth except Adam and Eve and
Cain and Abel, where did his wife come from? Why did
God reject Cain for displaying jealousy? Had He not forced
him to be jealous by giving obvious preference to Abel?

Whenever I asked these questions, I aroused indignation
for having the temerity to query God's omniscience and
omnipotence and for dismissing the information I did get
as illogical and inconsistent. Usually the response was evasive. I was told not to take the Bible so literally, that it was
symbolic. Symbolic of what? I asked, but got no answer. Or
I was reminded that the Bible contains much that is fine
and true, something that I had never denied; but I did not
see why I had to accept the things I found illogical.

Children want to be accepted and loved, so in the end
they do as they're told—which is precisely what I did. But

that did not mean that I had lost the need to understand. Unable to fathom God's motives, I set out more modestly to inquire into the motives people might have for so readily accepting these contradictions.

With the best will in the world I could find nothing evil in what Eve did. If God really loved those two he wouldn't want them to be blind, I thought. Was it really the serpent that seduced Eve into a desire for knowledge? Or was it God Himself? If an ordinary mortal were to show me something desirable and then say I must not desire it, I would find that positively perverse and cruel. But when it came to God, one wasn't even allowed to think such things, much less say them out loud.

So I was left alone with my reflections, and my search for enlightenment from books was equally fruitless. Then I made a simple discovery that put the contradictions in a whole new light. The Bible was written by men. We must assume that those men had been through some unpleasant experiences at the hands of their fathers. Surely none of them had had a father who took pleasure in their inquiring minds, realized the futility of expecting the impossible of them and refrained from punishing them. That was why they were able to create an image of God with sadistic features that did not strike them as such. God as they saw Him devised a cruel scenario in which He gave Adam and Eve the tree of knowledge but at the same time forbade them to eat its fruit—that is, to achieve awareness and become autonomous personalities. He wanted to keep them entirely dependent on Him.

To me, a father who takes pleasure in tormenting his child is sadistic. And punishing that child for the effects of his own sadism has nothing to do with love, but a great deal to do with poisonous pedagogy (the Bible is full of it). This was how the authors of the Bible saw their "loving" father. In his Epistle to the Hebrews (12:6–8), Paul makes it clear that it is chastisement that bestows the certainty of being the true sons of God and not bastards: "If ye endure chastening, God dealeth with you as with sons; for what son is he whom the father chasteneth not? But if ye be without chastisement, whereof all are partakers, then are ye bastards, and not sons."

I can imagine that people whose childhoods were lived in an atmosphere of respect, without physical punishment and humiliation, will believe in a different God when they grow up—a loving, guiding, explaining God, giving them an example they can live by. Either that or they may do without an idea of God altogether, preferring to get their bearings from human models they can look up to as embodiments of love in the true sense of the word.

This book is the expression of my identification with Eve. Not the infantile Eve palmed off on us as a kind of Little Red Riding Hood, easy prey to an animal's cunning temptation, but with an Eve who saw through the injustice of her situation, rejected the commandment "Thou shalt not know," set out to understand the difference between good and evil and was prepared to assume responsibility for her actions.

In these pages I offer the insights that have become accessible to me since I found the courage to listen to what my body was trying to tell me and in this way to decipher the meaning of the very beginning of my own life. The journey back through childhood to that beginning enabled me to discover and describe the subtle mechanisms of denial that operate in us but that we rarely perceive because the commandment "Thou shalt not know" gets in the way.

I sincerely believe that we not only have the right to know what is good and what is evil; we have the duty to acquire that knowledge if we hope to assume responsibility for our own lives and those of our children. Only by knowing the truth can we be set free. Only in this way can we free ourselves from the fears and anxieties we knew as children, blamed and punished for sins we did not know we had committed, the fateful fear of the sin of disobedience, that crippling anxiety that has wrecked so many people's lives and keeps them in thrall to their own childhood.

Given the right help, we as adults can free ourselves from that terrible spell. We can procure vital information and realize that we are no longer forced to stay the submissive child, searching for some profound logic in everything our educators and religious instruction teachers passed to us as the gospel truth—and which was nothing other than the product of their own anxieties. You will be amazed at the relief you will feel when you step out of that stifling role. Then, at last, you will claim your right to face reality head-on, to reject illogical justifications, and to remain true to your own history.

Part I

CHILDHOOD:

THE

UNTAPPED SOURCE

OF KNOWLEDGE

Alice Miller

Also by Alice Miller

Paths of Life
(1998)

Breaking Down the Wall of Silence
(1997)

Banished Knowledge
(1997)

The Drama of the Gifted Child
(completely revised edition, 1996)

The Untouched Key
(1992)

Pictures of a Childhood
(1996)

Thou Shalt Not Be Aware
(1985)

For Your Own Good
(1983)

$\mathcal{E}$ VER SINCE civilization began, people have debated how evil came into the world and what they can do to combat it. The prevailing view has held that evil results when a child's innate destructive instincts are not redirected into goodness, decency, and nobility of character by a liberal dose of corporal punishment.

Today, no one seriously believes in the old wives' tale that the devil smuggles a changeling into the cradle, forcing us to inflict a strict upbringing on the diabolical offspring to bend it toward submission. But from some quarters we do hear the serious contention that there are such things as genes that predispose certain individuals to delinquency. The quest for these rogue genes has inspired many a research project, even though the hypotheses behind it fly in the face of the facts. No advocate of the "congenital evil" theory has ever, for example, explained why suddenly, at the turn of the twentieth century, a spate of children with "bad genes" was born who would later be utterly willing to do Hitler's bidding.

Sufficient scientific evidence has been marshaled to re-
fute the notion that some people are just born bad. This absurd myth, encountered in almost all cultures, has been effectively exploded. It is dead, but it refuses to lie down. We
know today that the brain we are born with is not the finished product, as once thought. The structuring of the
brain depends very much on events experienced in the first
hours, days, and weeks of a person's life. And there is
mounting evidence that the brain is capable of being mod-
ified throughout life, and certainly in the early years. The
capacity for empathy, for example, cannot develop in the
absence of loving care. The child who grows up neglected,
emotionally starved, or subjected to physical cruelty will
forfeit this capacity.

Of course, we do not arrive in this world as a clean slate.
Every new baby comes with a history of its own, the history of the nine months between conception and birth. In
addition, children have the genetic blueprint they inherit
from their parents. These factors may determine what
kind of temperament a child will have, what inclinations,
gifts, predispositions. But character depends crucially upon
whether a person is given love, protection, tenderness, and
understanding in the formative years or exposed to rejection, coldness, indifference, and cruelty. Many very young
murderers, barely more than children, were born to adolescent, drug-dependent mothers—conditions that we

know often go along with extreme neglect, lack of attachment, and traumatization.

In recent years, neurobiologists have further established
that traumatized and neglected children display severe lesions affecting up to 30 percent of those areas of the brain
that control emotions. The explanation is that severe traumas inflicted on infants lead to an increase in the release of
stress hormones that destroy the newly formed neurons
and their interconnections.

In the scientific literature there is still next to no discussion of the implications of these discoveries for our understanding of child development and the delayed consequences of traumas and neglect. But this research confirms
what I described almost twenty years ago in *For Your Own
Good*, based not on experiment but on analytic work with
my patients and a close reading of historical educational
literature. In that work I quoted extensively from the man-
uals of the so-called *schwarze Pädagogik* ("poisonous pedagogy"), which insisted on the importance of drumming
the principles of obedience and cleanliness into babies in
the very first days and weeks of life. Studying this literature helped me understand what made it possible for individuals such as Adolf Eichmann to function like killer ro-
bots: they had accounts to settle dating back to their
earliest days. They had never been given the opportunity
to respond to the violence done to them in their youth.
Their destructive potential was the product not of

Freudian death drives but of the early suppression of their natural emotional reactions.

Books containing monstrous advice about "good" parenting to drill the baby into obedience, disseminated by educators like Daniel Gottlieb Moritz Schreber in Germany in the second half of the nineteenth century, went into as many as forty editions, so we can conclude that most parents read them and acted—in good faith—on their recommendations. They beat their children from the outset because they had been told this was the way to make them into decent members of society. The children thus treated did the same with their children.

They didn't know any different. Among that generation of traumatized children, some would become Hitler's adherents, adulators, and henchmen. In my view, it was the direct result of their early drilling. The cruelty they experienced turned them into emotional cripples, incapable of developing any empathy for the suffering of others. They had time bombs ticking away in their minds: they were unconsciously awaiting an opportunity to vent on others the pent-up rage inside them. Hitler gave them the scapegoats they needed.

The latest discoveries about the human brain might have been expected to bring about a radical change in our thinking about children and the way we treat them. But old habits die hard. It will take unequivocal legislation and large-scale informational campaigns before young parents will be able to free themselves of the burden of inherited "wisdom" and stop beating their children. Only then will it be all but impossible to give one's child a slap "inadvertently." Only then will the power of newly acquired knowledge get in the way of the hand raised to deal the "unthinking" blow.

These thoughts, which I have set out in much greater detail in my book *Paths of Life*, will perhaps suffice to suggest the immense significance I ascribe to the experiences undergone by infants in the first days, weeks, and months of their lives. To be sure, later influences can undo some of this damage, particularly for a traumatized or neglected child who encounters a helping or an enlightened witness. But such empathic individuals can be of real help only if they do not downplay the consequences of early deprivations. Unfortunately, such sensitivity is rare, even among so-called experts in the helping professions.

For a long time, the significance of the first few months of life for the later adult was a neglected subject even among psychologists. In several of my books I have tried to cast light on this area by discussing the lives of dictators such as Hitler, Stalin, Ceausescu, and Mao and demonstrating how they unconsciously reenacted their childhood situation on the political stage. Here, however, I want to turn my attention away from history and gaze instead at the present.

Are we so loath to tap the rich source of childhood because we know that frightening spirits lurk there? The reluctance is understandable, for as soon as we attempt to empathize with the situation a child is in, we are certain to encounter the ghosts that haunted our own childhoods. Many people would do anything to avoid confronting those spirits and having to experience themselves once again as small, helpless children. And yet an encounter of this kind can give them back the vitality and sensitivity that have been lost to them for a lifetime.

In the chapters that make up Part I, I illustrate the avoidance of childhood reality in six fields where we should expect precisely the opposite: medicine, psychotherapy, politics, the penal system, religion, and biography.

1

MEDICATION
VERSUS
MEMORY

I OFTEN SEE elderly persons in the pharmacy col-
lecting the pills and potions prescribed to them by
their family doctors. Sometimes I ask them whether their
doctors ever talk to them about their lives or only about
their illnesses. "What do you think?" they usually reply.
"There's no time for that kind of thing—there are dozens
of people in the waiting room. And what good would it do,
anyway? The main thing is he knows what's wrong with
me and what to do about it." Sometimes I persist and ask
whether there is anyone at all they can talk to about their
lives. "What are you driving at?" they ask. "When I was
younger I went out to work and had no time for talking.
Now that I do have the time, who'd be interested in hear-

ing the story of my life? When it comes down to it, you're on your own."

True, most of us are indeed on our own in that respect. But we would benefit tremendously from having someone to talk to about our childhoods, particularly when we get older. As our physical strength fades and we lose our youthful vigor, we are particularly susceptible to flashbacks to a time when we were helpless children. And that may be what makes us cling to a bagful of tablets in much the same way as we clung to our mothers for the help we urgently needed. Perhaps this symbolic substitute really does help in some cases. But it can never be a replacement for the presence of someone truly interested in our personal history. That kind of interest does not take up anywhere near as much time as we might think. We need an open door to our own past, an opportunity to take its very beginning seriously.

It is common knowledge that eating disorders are typically psychic in origin. But many doctors, not having learned to face up to their own emotions or gain access to their own childhoods, do not genuinely understand the language of the symptoms displayed by their patients suffering from such disorders. Failure to understand generates a feeling of powerlessness that has to be fended off quickly. How do we fend off feelings? Frequently by resorting to measures that will silence the language we cannot comprehend, thus making ourselves feel powerful

again instead of ineffectual. And how do we reduce symptoms to silence?

The possibilities are legion. Most of them take the form
of medication. In the case of eating disorders, elaborate di-
ets can give patients the illusion that the doctor is im-
mersed down to the smallest detail in their lives, their eating habits, their well-being. Minute supervision of eating
regimens in hospitals does in some cases bring about a
slight increase in body weight for anorexics. The psychological side effect of realizing that one is not some kind of
freak, that there are other people with the same problem,
can help these patients regain a bit of zest for life, perhaps
even some enjoyment in eating.

But this approach does not even address, let alone solve,
the main problems of anorexics: Why do they shy away
from life? Why can't they trust their families? Why must
they obsessively monitor their eating habits? Few hospitals
encourage or even allow an anorexic patient to ask: How
did I get this way? What's at the root of my illness? What
am I feeling? What am I trying to avoid? What kind of
nourishment do I really require? Yet in most cases the
source of these people's illnesses is a major breakdown in
communication, a profound and tragic form of distress often dating back to early childhood.

I once saw a television program on eating disorders that
portrayed four adolescent girls and wound up with a discussion by a panel of experts. All the physicians on the

panel agreed that anorexia was a medical mystery, that there was no way of determining where it came from. Nevertheless, they stressed, the situation was improving and it was important not to lose faith in the prospects for finding a cure.

The genuine improvements achieved in therapies that empower patients to experience and express their true emotions are never touted by either journalists or medical experts, no doubt because the people who have undergone such experiences are not invited to participate in televised discussions. Such lone voices are silenced by the fear of placing blame on parents. But only by overcoming that fear will we be able to understand a patient's emotions and history. And parents themselves will never learn to understand if they keep knowledge at arm's length for fear of the guilt it might arouse in them. Parents agonize over their children's symptoms and want to help them, but they do not know how. And doctors cannot afford the time to understand the motives of their patients—unless, that is, they themselves know by experience that facing up to accusations from their children will not have a lethal effect on parents. The worst thing such criticisms can do is to confront them with their own histories. And that kind of confrontation can sometimes motivate parents to start communicating with their children far more deeply than was possible before.

In the televised debate, the experts spoke of anorexia as if it were a purely physical phenomenon necessarily devoid of any other meaning. What they had to say no doubt appeared plausible enough to most viewers: a feeling of hunger can indeed disappear once a person has lost a certain amount of weight and sticks to a reduced diet low in minerals. The physiological and anatomical mechanisms behind a total loss of appetite are easy to understand. But they say nothing about its causes; they merely describe its mechanics.

What triggers anorexia in the first place is the tragedy of a young person unable to confide in anyone about her own feelings, to talk with anyone about how she needed to be nurtured as a child. Now she is unable, without help, to grasp the conflicts raging within her. In medical or psychiatric therapy she then encounters specialists equally concerned to evade such conflicts in themselves for fear that they might end up blaming their own parents. How can they hope to offer support to these young people? The patients can only summon the courage to put their discontent, their pain, their disappointment, their rage, and above all their needs into words if they are encouraged to do so by someone who does not share those fears or who has already experienced them and recognized them for what they are. There can be no doubt that successful therapeutic activity hinges on the therapist's own emotional development. The help provided by therapists, doctors, and social workers would take on a new dimension if knowledge of this childhood factor were widespread. So far, however, it appears to be taboo for the medical world.

Many people seeking help have realized the problem this issue represents for conventional medicine. But this awareness will not prevent them from falling prey to charlatans proposing all kinds of alternative methods, arousing hopes of a cure and sometimes even effecting a degree of relief where faith and hope turn out to be stronger than their patients' powers of judgment and knowledge of human nature. But what of those without this kind of faith who are tormented by physical symptoms? In many cases, working to recover one's own repressed and denied childhood brings genuine relief, especially to those with the good fortune to encounter enlightened witnesses who have gained emotional access to their own history.

For a long time I believed that learning to read the story of one's own childhood was something that could be achieved without the help of such witnesses, largely because I myself had no choice but to go my way, supported only by my writing and painting. But ultimately I was lucky enough to find an enlightened witness, and it was not until then that I was able to admit truths that I could never have borne on my own. Only then did I achieve the freedom I needed to take the messages from my body and my emotions completely seriously instead of questioning their validity.

But even for those who have not yet found an empathic therapist who has come to terms with his or her own childhood instead of projecting it onto clients, it can be helpful to tell someone about traumatic childhood experiences, as long as that person understands how those experiences can leave their mark on a child for life. Psychologist James W. Pennebaker, who describes the results of his studies in his book *Opening Up*, would appear to be an empathic listener. One of the many experiments he conducted took the form of asking students sitting in separate booths to report on painful experiences and to give free rein to the emotions that went with them. Another group was asked to describe events that hardly engaged their emotions, such as buying a pair of socks. The participants were students of psychology who were also undergoing outpatient treatment through the university health service. After the experiment Pennebaker established that those who had reported on emotionally charged events consulted their doctors at the health service less frequently than those who had recounted mundane occurrences.

From this study Pennebaker concluded—quite rightly, in my view—that a person's state of health will improve if he or she is given the opportunity to tell someone about distressing events, provided the listener shows interest and understanding. While this will hardly be sufficient to cure a severe illness like anorexia, it might have a salutary effect. But in encounters between doctors and their patients this opportunity is rarely taken. Doctors have little time to listen to their patients, and those who do take the time lack the necessary knowledge to understand the language of emotion. Probably the single most important factor militating against success is doctors' fear of reviving their own childhood traumas. Unfortunately, doctors frequently ward off such fears by diverting them onto their patients and instilling fear in them.

Isabelle, a fifty-year-old actress from Chicago, told me of her consultation with a specialist in internal disorders. She had been suffering from a chronic inflammation of the intestines that had set in immediately after a psychic shock she had endured. Isabelle was firmly convinced that she needed the help of another person to get to the bottom of her emotions and to understand why the illness had broken out suddenly and would not subside. Her temperature was normal, but she suffered from severe cramps, which she felt sure were the expression of her repressed emotional distress. Accordingly, she refused to take antibiotics. She had been to several other doctors, including homeopaths, all of whom had listened benevolently to the history of her problem and then prescribed medication.

Her new physician, Dr. Walker, appeared to justify her hopes of greater sympathy and understanding because he began by asking her about the most significant illnesses she had had in her life and listened with apparent interest to what she had to say. She succeeded in describing her central concerns within the space of ten minutes, and was pleased with herself. One of the threads running through the fabric of her whole life was the neglect of her psychic distress. Medication was considered the only remedy that could relieve the pain, yet she frequently suffered from the side effects without any easing of the symptoms themselves. Naturally, this merely served to increase the distress she felt.

Though she was in considerable pain, she refused medication because she was convinced that the pain would go away once she had understood the reasons for her illness. A number of her organs had already been removed; after each operation some other organ would immediately start causing her trouble and would persist until it, too, was removed. She was determined not to repeat that experience yet again.

The doctor listened to what she had to say and made notes. When she had finished, he reached for his pad and prescribed a three-week course of antibiotics. He said that she must embark on this treatment without delay if she did not want to risk cancer or another operation, which would probably involve the insertion of an artificial anus. Much alarmed by this verdict, Isabelle started to speak, but the doctor pointed to the clock and said there were lots of other patients waiting. He added that she was now fully informed about her condition and would only have herself to blame if she did not follow his instructions to the letter.

It is hardly surprising that in the days to come Isabelle's despair and physical pain became even worse. A series of blood tests she underwent at the recommendation of another doctor revealed nothing abnormal, nor did a sonogram of her intestines. Still refusing antibiotics, she found a psychotherapist with whom she could work on the emotional shock that had triggered her illness. There she was able to give free expression to her emotions and the strong feelings stemming, as she then recalled, from experiences in her childhood. After only a few weeks the intestinal symptoms began to fade as she gained an increasingly acute understanding of the way in which her illnesses were reflections of the plight she had gone through as a child.

It is not always possible to identify the complex causes of such an illness in the space of a few weeks or months. But when that does happen, the consequences are astounding. The indispensable requirement in all cases is the patient's willingness to embark on a journey of self-discovery. Of almost equal importance is the appreciation of the therapeutic prospects held out by such a method, the beneficial effects, so often ignored, of simply talking and listening.

I have singled out Isabelle's experience from among countless similar reports because it clearly delineates the dynamic that results when doctors mask their own fears and feelings of powerlessness to salvage their prestige. My impression is that the cogent description of the destructive role conventional medicine had played in Isabelle's life confronted Dr. Walker with a problem that he had perhaps never given any thought to and felt unable to address. At first he was prepared to listen to the patient's history of her illnesses because he expected her, like the majority of patients, to describe symptoms he had learned to treat in medical school. But Isabelle spoke of entirely different things: she described how medical treatment had occasioned the progressive *destruction* of her organs by subjecting her to operations that led only to more operations. No mention had been made in the doctor's medical education of how such destruction reflects the tragic history of a patient's childhood.

Do patients have any real defense against operations not only recommended but more or less forced on them as their only chance of survival? Where else are they to seek counsel? A person who has grown up in the company of parents able to come to grips with their fears and other emotions without passing them on to their children would immediately realize that the doctor was inadvertently foisting his own fears onto the patient. Such persons would have developed the capacity to see through unconscious manipulations. But such a person, having been allowed in childhood to articulate freely whatever caused her distress, would not be likely as an adult to suffer from chronic inflammation of the intestines. Typically, patients suffering from psychosomatic disorders were forced to develop a very different attitude in their early years: Ask no questions, shoulder other people's anxieties, tolerate contradictions, roll with the punches. And if they can find no one to guide them out of that rut, they may continue doing precisely that all their lives.

For Isabelle, the encounter with Dr. Walker was a turning point. What escaped him in her description was something that she herself realized. From then on, she knew with blinding clarity that it was up to her to take the necessary action. One could not expect a complete stranger, even a respected physician, to gain insight into her personal tragedy in the space of ten minutes. Neither his training nor his own motivation had equipped him to do so. Isabelle was the only one equal to deciphering the messages coming from her body. Recognizing that her symptoms were telling a story that reached back to her infancy, she knew that if she wanted to get to the heart of that story she needed someone to accompany her on her quest. On her own she would never be able to discover, let alone bear, the pain that small child had suffered. She would have to find a witness to whom she could say, "Look, this is what happened to me," and who would be prepared to take her seriously, having been through similar experiences in childhood. When Isabelle finally succeeded in finding such a person and spent several months engaging her total emotional energy in working through the shock she had suffered, she was able to identify the complete emotional loneliness in which she had spent her early childhood.

She had idealized her father for fifty years, but now, with the help of her therapist, she managed to accept the truth. In the first years of her life she had been sexually abused by her father, a successful dermatologist. Her mother did nothing to protect her. As she had been unable to confide her feelings to anyone, she frequently suffered from stomach aches and constipation. Her father's response was to give her frequent enemas, which she found very painful. He also ordered her to hold back the content of the enema for as long as possible. At a symbolic level the child took this to mean she must keep silent, remain alone with her pain, and yield to the violence done to her by her father. But the real injury, far from manifesting itself in frank brutality, was that her father ignored her personality. He degraded her, turning her into an object for gratifying his needs without caring in the slightest about the consequences his actions might have on her future life. One of those consequences was that Isabelle spent decades obeying her doctors in the same way she had obeyed her father.

As an educated woman, surely Isabelle could have found a doctor or therapist willing to listen to her, couldn't she? Today, she feels that she was unable to do so as long as she remained incapable of seeing what her father had done to her. She came to me after reading Marie-France Hirigoyen's *Stalking the Soul: Emotional Abuse and the Erosion of Identity*, in which she was convinced she had finally found the key to her life history. Isabelle had already been through a course of "classical" psychoanalysis which, though teaching her to call the "errors" of her parents by name, left her still unable to understand the bearing they had on her adult life.

Her intestinal problems, the many operations, and the eye-opening encounter with Hirigoyen's book made Isabelle realize that she would be destroying her own life if she went on trying to uphold her idealized image of her father and ignoring the signals emitted by her own body. In *Stalking the Soul* she found a description of a form of perversity her body was only too familiar with. But her mind refused to accept her father's true character. It was this refusal that made it necessary for her physical pain to persist until such time as Isabelle could summon the strength to face the truth.

Only after this discovery was she able to understand why she had found no one ready to sympathize with or even comprehend what she called her "shock experience." For behind the events she was trying to recount was the suffering of an infant, of the little girl before she was able to speak, entirely dependent on the understanding of adults and otherwise completely alone. Thus, although Isabelle felt the fierce pain of that shock, the full dimensions of the experience remained closed to her as long as she clung at all costs to her love for her father.

Outwardly, nothing spectacular had occurred—no heart attack, no accident, no event enlisting the immediate compassion of the people around her. What struck Isabelle full force was the realization that she was clinging to a pattern that was poisoning her life, her health, and her relationships and that something had to be done about it. For a clearer picture of how this came about, we need to look at the preliminary stages in greater detail.

The searing shock Isabelle experienced hit when her theater company was on tour in Dublin, where she had spent her childhood. She was planning to look up a friend from her youth, John, a man by whom she had always felt liked and understood. The two of them had lost contact thirty years before, when Isabelle emigrated to the United States. There, free at last, she was determined to forget as quickly as possible what she had been through in convent school: the canings, humiliations, constant supervision, and the dark room in which she had been locked up at any sign of rebellion. In America she married and had two sons, but soon afterward divorced. She rarely thought of John because she had cut all ties to Ireland. When she did remember him, though, it was with feelings of affection. Sometimes she wondered: Why didn't I stay with John? He really loved me. Have I run away from my own happiness?

In her mind's eye she still saw John as the diffident, dreamy young man who admired her and made no claims on her. Her present partner, Peter, was entirely different, always demanding personal confirmation from her and flying off the handle at the slightest frustration. Contrary to his usual custom, he did not accompany her on the Irish tour, so Isabelle was able to prepare herself for the encounter with the little Dublin girl fresh from convent school that she had once been. She wanted John to tell her how much he had sensed of the rage, fear, and loneliness she had felt at the time.

But John had not noticed anything. Meeting her again in Dublin, he even tried to talk her out of her memories. "You're mistaken," he said. "You were cheerful, lively, uninhibited—no one sensed any kind of suffering in you. Don't you remember the dances we went to, the concerts, the plays? You were so avid for life. I admired you so much."

Isabelle did not know—not yet, at least—why she was so disappointed. John was a kind man, and he was telling her the truth. All those years ago he had noticed only what she had let him notice. But the night after their reunion she awoke in her hotel room with dreadful pains in her abdomen. She dismissed the idea of calling a doctor because she knew that the pains were somehow connected with seeing John again. But she did not know what it was that had caused her such a shock. Only when she broke down in tears at dawn did the mental anguish come surging up to replace almost immediately the pains wracking her body. Finally she found the words to express what she was feeling. "Not even John saw what I was going through," she told me. "He only saw the carefree girl in me, the girl I sometimes was. But the rest of the time I was playing a role for him—and for myself. No one has ever seen me as

I am. I have always been completely alone with everything that hurts me." The expectation of finding an enlightened witness in John had been an illusion.

Isabelle wept in a way she had never wept before. So as not to be alone with her tears and pain, her first instinct was to call Peter, but she did not want to wake him. So she waited until daybreak in Chicago and then asked him if he could spare a moment to listen to her. She did not find it easy to ask Peter to listen; it was something she had never done before.

Her desperate need for a sign of sympathy from someone close to her made her throw all caution to the wind. Later she told me: "Of course, I needed someone to say they understood me because I couldn't understand it myself, I couldn't see why such a petty reason should have unleashed such floods of tears in me. But even if he hadn't been able to understand, it would have done me good for Peter just to say something nice to me. But all I got from him was a barrage of cruel accusations. He was obviously completely unable to cope with my call. He asked me what I meant by springing this on him without warning. He was just off to work, and as a lawyer he would be spending all day listening to other people's troubles. I was indulging in histrionics. Didn't I have enough drama on the stage without bringing it all into real life? Hadn't he tried to dissuade me from going on this journey? But I never listened to him. Anyway, it was quite normal for someone going back to the place they were born to be assailed by old memories. It would soon blow over."

After the call Isabelle did what she always did: she tried her best to understand the situation Peter was in, his inability to cope with her feelings, possibly because their intensity frightened him. But her body refused to cooperate. It immediately signaled its disappointment by more cramps, this time so painful she had no choice but to call a doctor, who gave her some homeopathic medication. Despite the sleepless night she had spent, she managed to go onstage and perform that evening, but her exhaustion and grief were so great that she left for home the very next day. Back in Chicago, the pains reasserted themselves and she became chronically ill. She consulted doctor after doctor, swallowed countless pills and potions, and finally chanced on the psychotherapist in whose company she was able to recognize what her father's abuse of her as a child had done to her as an adult.

I do not believe that the mere realization of the incestuous abuse and the strong feelings it involved would have been sufficient to cure Isabelle. The essential thing was that it made a number of other discoveries and decisions possible. It trained a searchlight on the relationships with men she had had up to that point, all of them marked by this early abuse and the suspicion and mistrust born of it. It also enabled her to rethink her relationship to Peter.

The shock she experienced in Dublin and Peter's dismissive, unsympathetic response brought home to her how much she had suffered when the men in her life had ignored her real self. But she was also able to see how much she had contributed to their response by concealing her real self from them and playing a part. For John she was the uncomplicated, cheerful companion of his youth, for her ex-husband and Peter she was an available object making no apparent claims on them. As for her two sons, such behavior derived quite naturally from her role as mother. But there alone, in her relationship with her children, a relationship where availability to others would indeed have been the right thing, she sometimes claimed the right to refuse others emotional access to her, something her sons found impossible to understand and very painful. Only in her work was Isabelle able to express feelings, but tragically they were the feelings of another person, whomever she was portraying onstage. She herself had no right to her own identity. As a child she had been refused that right, and she went on denying it to herself for fifty years.

The merciless abdominal pains ravaging Isabelle's body after her reunion with John confronted her with questions: Who am I really? Why am I not really there in all my relationships? I suffer when others fail to see me as I am, but how can they see me if I don't show myself, if I conceal my true nature from them? And what makes me do that?

Later, in therapy, she found an answer to these questions. She gradually realized that she had been forced, perhaps since birth, to develop a strategy to protect herself
from the pain of a child never perceived by her parents as
a person in her own right, merely used to gratify their own
needs. To evade that pain, Isabelle had learned to banish
her own needs and feelings, to hide them from herself and
others, to be absent, nonexistent. Today, she says that it was
as if she had killed herself. She now believes that in childhood she actually split her own personality.

In therapy Isabelle came to understand that she did precisely that when she was sexually abused by her father. She
had learned to conceal her true personality from the person
she loved, the person inflicting profound harm on her because his caresses were not meant for her as a person. Now,
at age fifty, she was able to look me in the eye and declare:

"I feel the need to say this out loud and to say this to
you as the author of *Thou Shalt Not Be Aware*. For him
my body was nothing other than an object for mastur-
bating on. Can you imagine how you feel when you realize that? Not for one second did he think of the way he
was destroying my life, because for him I simply did not
exist as a person, a human being with feelings of my
own. It still hurts to say that, but it was crucial for me to
free myself of the delusion that my father loved me. The
first time I consciously felt that pain was when John told

me that he had always seen in me the carefree girl he took me for. Now I'm glad for that night in Dublin. After all, I still have some of my life left, and I intend to exorcise that curse. I don't need to hide any more, because I no longer need to protect myself from things that have already happened. As long as I so thoroughly denied that fact, I invariably chose partners who didn't really mean *me* when they took up with me. I've stopped playing the good little girl. I've stopped looking for my true self in the roles I play onstage. I have finally dared to be what I am and to live my own life. And the abdominal pains have gone away."

When Freud discovered, more than a hundred years ago, that neuroses are frequently traceable to the repression of incest experiences, he thought it was sufficient to break down that repression and denial (through hypnosis if necessary) in order to bring the patient back to mental health. But as this failed in most cases to produce a cure, he discarded his hypothesis about the origins of neurosis being rooted in the denial of traumatic childhood experience and developed his psychoanalytic method, which builds on the rejection of that hypothesis.

In my view, Isabelle's story helps us understand why most of Freud's female patients did not achieve a breakthrough. It is not sufficient to desist from repression (and certainly not under hypnosis, which often willfully disregards defense barriers) in order to free oneself from very early survival strategies and open up the path on which the cruelly deceived child can find the way back to trusting others. Education and encouragement are not enough to give the child hidden away in an adult the courage to assert the self—not as long as the body remains alone with its knowledge. Only the discovery of the truth and the logical consistency of those infant strategies will make it possible for adults to free themselves of those strategies and their all but automatic repetitions in the present. And this can only happen in the security afforded by a relationship with an enlightened witness.

The process of healing requires both the confrontation with childhood traumas and the uncovering of the numerous defense mechanisms that have been erected to protect the child from unbearable pain and distress. Given the right therapeutic approach, adults can achieve both those aims.

Isabelle realizes that the expectations she placed in Dr. Walker were much too much for him, but she does feel he could have helped her if he had said something like, "You seem to be on the right track. The intestines are very sensitive and frequently respond to mental distress with cramps. Try talking to an expert about the shock you've been through. That can do a great deal of good."

I am convinced that many operations and tragedies could be avoided if more doctors were capable of displaying such an attitude instead of ignoring their patients' personal histories. No one expects a specialist in internal disorders to find a solution in a case as complicated as Isabelle's, or to identify not only the emotional factors behind her symptoms but the soil in which those emotions grew in her childhood. But Dr. Walker might have helped Isabelle find a solution if he had respected his own limits and had some inkling of psychosomatic medicine. Instead he was content to exercise his power and delegate his own anxieties to his patient.

This chapter is not in any sense intended to advocate alternative medicine. All I wish to show is that the medical profession can benefit from incorporating childhood reality into medical training instead of ignoring it. This applies equally, of course, to psychotherapy.

2

EVADING
CHILDHOOD
REALITY IN
PSYCHOTHERAPY

---

*C*OMMON WISDOM may hold that psychotherapists concern themselves with the childhoods of their clients, but this is by no means always true. Various psychotherapeutic schools of thought consciously phase childhood out of their work or touch on it only when they have no other option. Many therapists believe that exploring childhood is actively harmful because clients will then experience themselves as victims instead of responsible adults.

I, too, firmly believe that adults are responsible for their actions, and that only in childhood were they helpless victims. But I also believe that owning up to their early histories can help them understand why they still *feel and act as if they were helpless victims*. Psychotherapy can give them an understanding of the processes involved, which in turn can help them abandon the victim posture. There are said to be people whom behavior therapy has helped banish their anxieties. They are to be most warmly congratulated. Many others, however, are unable to profit from such an approach. They are also unable to free themselves from depression with the help of medication because their urge to find out who they are and why they have become the way they are might be stronger in them than the wish to be free of depression.

For these people, work on their own childhoods can be a rich source of insight. It is highly regrettable that psychiatric training today places the main emphasis on administering medication. Of course, it is easy to appreciate that a patient will find regular doses of dopamine an immense relief if his or her brain is not producing that substance. But that does not explain why the substance is lacking. And the answer to that question might just be the key to a genuine and lasting cure. Medication can be temporarily helpful, particularly if the patient is not interested in exploring the causes of the condition. But many psychiatrists resort to medication even in cases where such exploration would have been possible.

I do not support the current tendency to reinforce psychotherapy with medication. Most such medications interfere with clients' interest in their childhoods or leave them even more in the dark about their own past reality than they were before, thus undermining the potential success of psychotherapy. Even some psychiatrists who specialize in treating people suffering from post-traumatic disorders, people who experienced severe traumas in adulthood, don't necessarily work with these patients on their childhood. Yet it is logical, and has been scientifically confirmed, that a person who grew up in a relatively healthy family will be more likely to overcome later psychic trauma (such as results from a plane accident or a physical assault) better than somebody who was mistreated in childhood. Working with that person on his whole history may thus lead to better results.

In one family I know, the mother, Jean, suffered from severe recurrent depression over a period of twenty years and was confined to bed on various occasions because she refused to eat and did not have the strength to get up. Countless doctors treated her for this condition, some with medication, others with talk therapy. Sporadic remissions alternated with relapses of frightening severity. Once I met her husband, Tom, and asked how she was. He said, despairingly, that he could hardly bear to see how she was destroying herself. I asked him if she had found out anything about her childhood in the various therapies she had been through. "God forbid!" he exclaimed. "It would kill her if she did!" He knew her parents, and both of them had been tyrannical with their daughter.

When I called sometime later, I was immediately struck by a change in Jean's voice. She told me that she had been free of depression for a year, although business prospects (the couple ran a travel agency) were anything but rosy. She had found a therapist who, instead of giving her medication, asked her to talk about her childhood. Though this was hard for her, she felt there was someone at her side throughout, and thus she finally succeeded in discovering the origins of her illness. She felt much stronger, had put on weight, and was happy that she could "feel herself" instead of being alienated from herself by medication. She did not know that I had been a psychotherapist myself, nor had she read any of my books. What she told me was entirely spontaneous.

"Just imagine," Jean said, "I spent years tormenting my own body, destroying my zest for life, spoiling every pleasure I might have had, and insisted on clinging to the idea that my parents loved me. The therapy exploded those illusions, and I now know what price I paid. Amazingly, my strength has come back, I can look after myself, and I've stopped being a victim to the exclusion of all else. I now see that I treated myself very cruelly for years and years without knowing what I was doing."

This woman had been treating her body in precisely the way her parents had treated her as a child. It was not allowed any pleasure in life, it had to obey her commands and almost collapsed under the pressure. She was allowed no awareness, no understanding of what was happening, no realization that she was a victim of the tragic history of her parents, who themselves had been terrorized as children. Depression and anorexia doomed their daughter to vegetating in a carefully erected structure of self-delusion rather than living a real life. As had all the doctors and psychiatrists she had been to, her husband, who loved her and wanted to help her, believed that she must be spared the truth, that she was too weak to stand up to it. But it was precisely the truth that saved her. Freed from the necessity to lie to herself, she found the strength to see her parents' destructive behavior for what it was and to break the cycle of repeating it.

In his book *Love and Survival*, the cardiologist Dean Ornish tells us that heart patients living in resilient partner relationships have better survival rates than unattached patients. Though he is certainly right when he says that love is the best medicine, the mere fact of living in a family rather than on one's own tells us nothing about the capacity for love that a particular person may have. Jean, though truly loved by her husband and daughter, was unable to find access to her true feelings and needs, and so was for all intents and purposes alone. She was in a state of constant conflict with the knowledge her body possessed but her conscious mind refused to accept. She had a loving and lovable husband, and she desperately wanted to love him just as much as she loved her daughter. But her capacity for love was stunted by the war going on inside her. Only when she resolved to face the truth was she able to overcome that inner barrier.

With all due respect for everything that has been said and written about the power of love, we should never forget that good will and devout wishing alone will not be enough to free a person to love if that person is in a state of unremitting internal war. This desperate conflict would not be taking place if that person's true self had not been suppressed in childhood.

Psychotherapy is a viable way, indeed the most promising way, of discovering the causes of a person's tragic development. But for that to happen, the client must really want it and the therapist must already have been through the experience in order to navigate past the hazards that lie in the way. It is neither advisable nor necessary for every patient to lapse into a state of profound regression; sometimes even momentary glimpses of childhood reality can have a therapeutic effect, as long as the feelings that go with them are experienced in the presence of an enlightened witness. Facing them alone would almost certainly lead to renewed traumatization.

Working on present problems will invariably uncover traces of early wounds inflicted by a traumatic childhood. Gradually a picture emerges in which clients can identify

the way they were programmed for anxiety, self-subjuga-
tion, self-denial, and blindness, and then set about freeing
themselves from that program. Without this discovery, the
apparent liberation brought about by methods such as neurolinguistic programming and behavior therapy, which em-
ploy self-manipulation, will be temporary. The positive effect may last some time—under favorable circumstances
even a very long time—but such therapies will not root out
the urge to repeat the traumatic experience of childhood on
oneself, one's children, or other people. As soon as the external circumstances take a turn for the worse, this compulsive repetition can regain its old strength, and no acquired
technique of self-manipulation will be able to resist it.

How could it be otherwise if our bodies know the whole
story but house a spirit determined to control and lay down
the law, just as our parents did in the first few months of
our lives? The body must then submit and obey, but from
time to time it can signal its distress through symptoms,
just as a child may do by performing poorly in school, constantly falling ill, or presenting the parents with mystify-
ing behavior. But the more strongly the parents' urge to exercise power manifests itself as a way of covering over
their own helplessness, the more enigmatic the language
of the child's symptoms becomes. Ultimately, there is no
hope of any genuine communication. Only when the parents give up their bid for power can the child's distress find
a voice. We will not get very far if we try to escape the

truth we are carrying within us. The denied truth will be with us wherever we flee. It will cause us pain, prompt us to do things we will regret, increase our confusion, and weaken our self-confidence. But if we face up to it, we have a chance of finally recognizing what happened, what didn't happen, and what has forced us to end up living our lives in opposition to our most profound needs.

The lives of people seriously harmed in early childhood are never simple. Jean, for example, relapsed into severe depression when she and Tom were forced to move out of the house where she had grown up. Some of her old symptoms returned. Fortunately, she was able to find meaning in them and to get her bearings without having to fear a major disaster. But such anxieties cannot be dissipated if clients sense their therapists' fear of their own childhoods. They will identify with that instead of seeking as adults to *fathom* their childhoods. They will merely end up *reliving* the panic of their traumatic early years without understanding it fully. Only systematic work on the history of their childhoods can give clients a frame of reference that will enable them constantly to improve their understanding of the crippling fears beginning to surface and to recognize their origins.

Brigitte, a colleague in training, told me a story that illustrates the points I have been making. She has permitted me to recount it here, with some changes of incidental details. A colleague, Henry, told her that Roger, the director of

an institution organizing foster care for abused children,
had been put on trial for sexual abuse. She then got in touch
with Roger, who gave her the particulars of the case. A foster family, Roger told her, had been exploiting the child entrusted to its care. Initially, as head of the institution that
had made the assignment, Roger had been called to account, but subsequently he was exonerated of any wrong-
doing. But he was so furious at the rumor that he was still
under suspicion that he decided to threaten to sue Henry for
defamation. When Henry received Roger's letter, he immediately relapsed into the pattern inherited from his childhood. Henry's first move was to call Brigitte and confront
her with the fruits of his disastrous upbringing. He knew,
he said, that she had always had something against him and
that she was now doing her best to ruin him completely.
When she asked whether he recalled giving his consent to
further inquiries, he shouted into the phone, "I'm not talking to you anymore. I'm appalled and disgusted by what
you've done." She asked whether he would not have done
the same in her position. "I'd never have done anything so
terrible," he roared, and then reiterated, "I'm not talking to
you anymore." She replied that he must have wanted to talk
to her, otherwise he wouldn't have called in the first place.
"No," he said, "I wanted to give you a piece of my mind. I
refuse to talk to anyone like you."

Brigitte had the impression that what she was hearing
was the ranting of a furious father not allowing the child

he was browbeating to get a word in edgewise. She concluded that such treatment must have been meted out to Henry on many occasions.

But might Henry genuinely not be aware of this? Both of them were psychiatrists undergoing therapeutic training. Brigitte was amazed at this uncontrolled outbreak of rage and at Henry's inability to realize that he had brought the situation on himself. She explained the ease with which he made her a target of his attacks as a case of regression in which he was transferring onto her the rage he felt at his mother for not protecting him from a violent father. His perception of present reality was badly awry; otherwise the reality of his childhood and the panic of the beaten child would not have been so promptly triggered by Roger's threat. His overwhelming panic made him unable to think straight and to perceive his own responsibility. At the end of the exchange Brigitte managed to get in the following words: "You treat me as if I were an enemy, but I'm not. I hope you'll realize that when you've calmed down a little."

The next day Henry called again, totally transformed. His therapist had helped him write a friendly letter to Roger, disclosing the names of the two people who had misinformed him and apologizing. He also asked Brigitte's forgiveness for laying into her as he had. He said he didn't know what had come over him but he had been working too hard recently. Brigitte attempted to communicate her feelings, telling him how she had felt like a child trying to justify the parents' actions, reminding them of what they had said but not being allowed to speak up. She said she knew of such situations from her own experience and from what her clients told her. "I know," said Henry. "You put everything down to childhood. But my outburst had nothing to do with my childhood, though I did get beaten a lot. My therapist thinks I went for you like that because you're a woman, so I was less afraid of you than I was of the man who was threatening me."

Though glad that it had come to a good end, Brigitte could not get over what she had experienced. To her it had been evident that Henry had relapsed into the reality of his childhood when he blew his top during the first phone call. It may well be, she thought, that he was frequently harried into panic situations by an uncontrolled father who never let him finish what he was saying. And it may be that he could only keep his head above water by flailing out at his mother. Seconded by a therapist offering him feminist interpretations while excluding childhood from the process altogether, Henry was letting himself be overpowered by his emotions without achieving any understanding of them.

I could quote many similar behavior patterns. I have caught myself lapsing into such denial mechanisms on several occasions. But therapists must never share in a patient's denial. With the right kind of training, they will be able to see behind the patient's damaging or self-damaging outbursts, identify the childhood realities lurking there, and present the patient with them. Everyone has barriers; finding out about them is one reason we consult a therapist. Therapists have the usual human limitations but not the same barriers as patients, so they can help gradually break down the barriers and remove their stubborn effects.

Brigitte's example shows that even budding psychotherapists who themselves are undergoing analysis evade the topic of traumatization inflicted by humiliation and cruelty in childhood. It is understandable that Henry, on his own admission frequently beaten in childhood, should not be able to expose himself to those feelings without the right therapeutic encouragement. So it is doubly regrettable that he was being analyzed by a therapist who encouraged him in his evasions.

Henry's therapist should have been able to appreciate the risk Henry was running by letting himself be driven by a rage he was unable to control because he was unable to direct and understand it, attacking or slandering people who had done nothing to him. To Brigitte, well acquainted with the thought patterns of poisonous pedagogy, it was obvious that Henry was adopting the pattern of one (or both) of his parents, blaming and laying into the child and not letting him say what he had to say. Conceivably, Henry might have responded to what Brigitte had said to him—it might have given him food for thought. But his therapist confirmed him in his assumption that his acting out had nothing to do with his childhood. Thus therapy may cement the patient's private denial, and Henry may end up treating his own patients the same way. There is nothing to free him from the compulsion to reproduce the pattern he learned from his parents. Once he has become a therapist himself, his patients will all enter into this perpetual cycle of compulsive repetition. None of them will be allowed to profit from the opportunities modern psychotherapy can offer when patients are given the chance to understand the repressed emotions of early childhood in their proper context.

3

CORPORAL
PUNISHMENT
AND POLITICAL
MISSIONS

---

*U*NDER CERTAIN circumstances, children who have been told repeatedly that the humiliations and beatings they have been subjected to are for their own good may end up believing it all their lives. Consequently they will raise their own children in the same way, laboring under the delusion that they are doing the right thing. But what happens to all the rage, the pain, the anger those children were forced to suppress when they were not only treated cruelly by their own parents but expected to be grateful for it?

Tackling this question has helped me get nearer to an-
swering the first of the questions I asked about childhood:
How does evil come into the world? Gradually the conviction took shape in my mind that evil is re-produced with
each new generation. Newborn infants are innocent.
Whatever predispositions they may have, they feel no urge
or need to destroy life. They want to be looked after and
protected, to love and be loved. If those needs are not satisfied, if children are abused instead of cherished, then
that will determine the entire course of their lives. Human
beings feel the urge to be destructive only if they were subjected to cruelty at the beginning of their own lives. A
child who has been loved and respected will have no motivation to wage war on others. Evil is not an inevitable or
integral part of human nature.

Although these insights seemed logical and consistent to
me, I still had my doubts because hardly anyone seemed to
agree with me. To prove to myself that my convictions
were true, I turned my attention to the life of Adolf Hitler.
I thought that if I could show that this monstrous mass
murderer was made into what he was by his parents, it
would be the end of the traditional idea that some people
are just "born bad." I described Hitler's childhood in my
book *For Your Own Good,* and many of my readers were
aghast. One woman wrote: "If Hitler had had five sons he
could have vented his revenge on for the tortures he was

subjected to in his childhood, then he would probably never have victimized the Jewish people. You can take everything you've suffered out on your own children and never get punished because murdering the soul of your own child can always be passed off as parenting, child-raising, upbringing." In *Paths of Life* (pp. 158–161) I elaborated on the childhood roots of Hitler's hatreds:

We know that as a boy Hitler was tormented, humiliated, and mocked by his father, without his mother being able to protect him. We also know that he denied his true feelings toward his father. . . . This hatred remained repressed because hating one's father was strictly prohibited, and because it was in the interests of the child's self-preservation to maintain the illusion of having a good father. Only in the form of a deflection onto others was hatred permitted, and then it could flow freely.

Hitler's specific problems with the Jews can in fact be traced back to the period before his birth. In her youth, his paternal grandmother had been employed in a Jewish merchant's household in Graz. After her return home to the Austrian village of Braunau, she gave birth to a son, Alois, later to become Hitler's father, and received child-support payments from the family in Graz for fourteen years. This story, which is recounted in many biographies of Hitler, represented a dilemma for

the Hitler family. They had an interest in denying that
the young woman had been left with child either by the
Jewish merchant or his son. On the other hand, it was
impossible to assert that a Jew would pay alimony for so
long without good reason. Such generosity on the part of
a Jew would have been inconceivable for the inhabitants
of an Austrian village. . . .

For Alois Hitler, the suspicion that he might be of
Jewish descent was insufferable in the context of the
anti-Jewish environment he grew up in. . . . The only
thing he could do with impunity was to take out this rage
on his son Adolf. According to the reports of his daughter Angela, he beat his son mercilessly every day. In an
attempt to exorcise his childhood fears, his son nurtured
the maniac delusion that it was up to him to free not only
himself of Jewish blood but also all Germany and later
the whole world. Right up to his death in the bunker,
Hitler remained a victim of this delusion because all his
life his fear of his half-Jewish father had remained
locked in his unconscious mind.

Jews were not the only target of Hitler's rage and fear.
He was also frightened by the chaotic behavior of his
schizophrenic aunt, Johanna, who lived with the family:

As an adult, Hitler ordered every handicapped and
psychotic person to be killed, to free the German society

from this burden. Germany seemed for him to symbolize the innocent child who had to be saved.

Besides his fears in connection with his father and aunt, there was his early relationship with his very intimidated mother, who lived in constant fear of her husband's violent outbursts and beatings.

These irrational fears—which an outsider watching his speeches on video can easily recognize—remained unrecognized and unconscious to Hitler until the end of his life. Stored up in his body, they drove him constantly to new destructive actions in his endless attempt to find resolution.

Not all my readers were able to accept this view of Hitler and concede that his terrifying example demonstrates how evil comes about, how tiny, innocent children can turn into ravening beasts threatening not only their own families but the whole world. I was reminded that many children get beaten and otherwise abused in childhood, but they do not all turn into mass murderers. I took these arguments seriously and investigated the question of how children can survive brutal treatment without becoming criminals later in life. From a close study of many biographies, I established that in those cases where the victim did not turn into a victimizer, there was invariably some figure that had shown the child affection, the person I call the helping witness. Children with helping witnesses to turn to were able to gain awareness of the evil that had been done to them while at the same time identifying with the person who had shown them kindness. The Russian novelist Fyodor Dostoyevsky is one well-known example. Though he probably suffered at the hands of his brutal father, he was given solace by his loving mother.

Children with no helping witness are in the greatest danger of regarding the dreadful things they have been subjected to as for their own good and then dealing out to others the same kind of treatment without the slightest pangs of conscience. In short, they will ideologize this hypocrisy. Hitler the child learned at home that blows and humiliations were right and proper. Hitler the adult insisted—and believed—that it was his calling to save Germany by exterminating the Jews. Other dictators have ideologized their acts of vengeance in similar ways. Stalin *had to* purge Russia of the subversive "cosmopolitans"; Napoleon *had to* establish the *Grande Nation*, cost what it might; Milosevic *had to* make Serbia into a great nation.

Society's blindness to these mechanisms is what still makes wars possible, *because the actual reasons behind them remain in the dark*. Although probably all historians, at least in Germany, know very well that Frederick the Great was humiliated and tormented by his father, I have yet to come across a historical work that makes the connection between the cruelty meted out to this sensitive child and the monarch's later compulsive urge to overthrow as many countries as he could. Obviously this subject is still taboo.

For as long as we have recorded memory, the same woeful picture has been repeating itself. Men go off to war, women cheer them as they leave, and very few question what really sparked it off. Wars patently designed to invade and conquer foreign territory are passed off as acts of self-defense, or as the fulfillment of some holy mission. Most people are blind to the genuine reasons behind these "missions." Only when we have understood where evil comes from and how we keep it alive in our children will we cease to be helplessly exposed to its effects. We have a long way to go.

In nearly half of the fifty states in the United States, teachers are still allowed to spank children in school. This punishment is given for minor offenses, usually in the form of paddling on the buttocks performed by a person specially designated to do so. There is a graded scale of different forms of corporal punishment aimed at meting out "discipline." Pupils are made to stand in a corridor awaiting their turn to be chastised. These children appear to consider this institutionalized humiliation as something normal. Only later will their pent-up feelings of rage be vented in acts of criminal aggression. Most parents tolerate this system; some actively endorse it. Isolated mothers and fathers who oppose it are more or less doomed to ineffectuality. In Texas alone, according to the Project NoSpank Web site (http://www.nospank.org), some 118,000 children are punished this way each year.

Many teachers cannot imagine a school system entirely free of such punishment. They themselves grew up in an atmosphere of violence, so they learned very early to believe in the effectiveness of punitive measures. Neither in their own childhood nor during their teacher training were they given the chance to develop a sensitivity to the sufferings of children. Thus they have little awareness that, in the long run, using physical force against children merely teaches them to behave aggressively later in life.

Children with a background of domestic violence have learned to devote all their attention to averting danger. So they will hardly be able to concentrate on what they are being taught at school. They may well expend most of their energies on observing the teacher so as to be prepared for the physical "correction" that they feel to be inevitable. If it does come, it will reinforce their view. On the other hand, a teacher who understands these children's fears might move mountains—provided, again, that the abused child's reality is never played down.

We come across the same phenomenon in politics. As long as we are unaware of the degree to which the right to human dignity was denied us in childhood, it will not be easy to concede that right to our own children, however sincerely we may want to do so. Frequently we believe we are acting in the interests of the children and fail to realize we may be doing the very opposite, simply because we have learned to be callous in this respect at such an early stage. The effects of that learning are stronger than all the things we may learn later.

We can see an illustration of this in present-day legislation. As of September 2000, the German parliament has expressly denied natural parents the right to physical correction. As recently as 1997 they were still entitled to that questionable privilege; it was denied only to non-blood relatives and other caregivers. The overwhelming majority (80 percent) of German parliamentarians were convinced at the time that in certain cases corporal punishment at the hands of the natural parents could have a salutary effect. This opinion is still shared by most legislators, as recent decisions in Britain show. The persistent argument was that physical force should not be prohibited because it prepares children for life's dangers and thus helps them learn to protect themselves.

But beaten children are not learning how to defend themselves against criminals. They are learning to fear their parents, to play down their own pain, and to feel guilty. Being subjected to physical attacks that they are unable to fend off merely instills in children a gut feeling that they do not deserve protection or respect. This perniciously false message is stored in their bodies and will influence their view of the world and their attitude toward their own children. They will be unable to defend their claim to human dignity, unable to recognize physical pain as a danger signal and act accordingly. Their immune sys-

tems may even be affected. In the absence of other persons
on whom to model their behavior, these children will see
the language of violence and hypocrisy as the only effective means of communication. Naturally, they will avail
themselves of that language when they grow up because
adults normally suppress feelings of powerlessness and
helplessness. This is the real reason why so many defend
the old system of parenting and schooling.

In Cameroon an organization named EMIDA (*Elimi-
nation de la maltraitance infantile domestique africaine*) reports that it has statistical evidence suggesting that 218
million children in Africa are regularly subjected to physical "correction." When I inquired about the reasons for
such a high incidence of maltreatment, I was told it is a
common myth that the brain functions better when children are beaten until they bleed. It is understandable that
when they reach adulthood, children brought up in such a
tradition will adhere to this system so as to avoid confronting their repressed early suffering. But the consequences of such repression are all too apparent in the
bloody clashes between the peoples of Africa. All kinds of
reasons are advanced to explain these conflicts, but the
most plausible one is the pent-up rage of the beaten child
thirsting for release and vengeance.

I have frequently asked myself how something so terrible as the massacres in Rwanda could come about.

Rwandan children are customarily carried on their mothers' backs and breast-fed until quite a late age, a fact that we are inclined to interpret as indicating idyllic conditions of loving care rather than a breeding ground for maltreatment. Only recently did I receive information that brought home to me how high a price these children had to pay for the love of their mothers. They are conditioned to obey at a very early age. They are smacked for fouling their mothers' backs with their excrement. Fear of these spankings causes them to cry as soon as they feel the urge to excrete, thus warning the mother in time to take the child off her back and impress on it the need for cleanliness.

As a result of this conditioning the babies are "clean" at a very early age, and much the same methods are used to ensure that they stay quiet. I feel that the massacres in Rwanda may well be traceable to this abuse of babies. Though children in all African schools are cruelly beaten (in a survey conducted by EMIDA in 2000, only twenty out of more than two thousand children responding said that they were never beaten at home or at school), the methods used on infants are the ones that are of decisive importance. The earlier the use of violence starts, the more profoundly the lesson is internalized and the less accessible it is to later control by the conscious mind. Thus the first opportunity, in the form of some kind of political ideology, will suffice to spark off bestial cruelty in quiet, servile people who were living with explosive suppressed aggression.

For those acts of vengeance society provides a whole range of ideological guises. Racism, anti-Semitism, fundamentalist fanaticism, and "ethnic cleansing" are only some of them. Many young people engaged in such activities strongly believe that they are serving idealistic aims.

4

PRISONERS:
TIME BOMBS IN
THE BRAIN

---

*I*N NO REALM is the entrenched ignorance about childhood reality more virulent than in the penal system. Today's penitentiaries may have little in common with the grim fortresses of past centuries, but on one point nothing seems to have changed: the questions of why people turn criminal and what they can do to avoid falling back into the same trap over and over again are hardly ever asked. If it were, prisoners would need to be encouraged to think about what happened to them in childhood, to write it all down and disclose it to others in the framework of a structured therapy group.

In my last book, *Paths of Life*, I reported on one such program in Canada. Thanks to the work done there, a number of fathers who had sexually abused their daughters were able to fathom for the first time the suffering they had inflicted on their children. Encouraged to talk about their own childhoods with people they had learned to trust, they came to understand that they had been passing on something that they themselves had experienced very early in their lives.

We are accustomed to keeping silent about childhood suffering, and because of this silence we often do things blindly. Talking liberates prisoners from their blindness, giving them access to awareness and protecting them from mindless acting out. Unfortunately, programs like the one in Canada are the exception. The prisons are full of people with time bombs ticking away in their brains, bombs that urgently need to be defused. With more knowledge and awareness this goal would be entirely feasible.

In 2000 the French novelist Emmanuel Carrère published an unusual book. *L'Adversaire* tells the true story of a man of above-average intelligence who studied medicine twenty years ago but never took the obligatory exam after the second year of medical school and so was unable to continue his studies. But he kept up the pretense of carrying on with his training and finally of having passed his exams. "Dr. Romand" married, had two children, and told his wife and friends that he was involved in a research project for the World Health Organization in Geneva. He left the house every morning for his "office" but in reality spent the day sitting in cafés, reading magazines, or studying travel brochures. This went on for eighteen years. Occasionally he stayed away for a few days on "research trips," spending the time at hotels. He was kind to his family, often dropped the children off at school, and was generally thought to be a model father.

His parents and parents-in-law had entrusted him with large sums of money, which they had asked him to invest for them in Switzerland. But he used the money to support his family. On one occasion he was alone in the house with his father-in-law, who told him he was contemplating buying a Mercedes and intended to withdraw some of the money he had given him to invest. That same day the old man had a fatal "accident," a fall down a flight of stairs. Later a woman friend also announced that she required a large sum of money from the account he was supposed to have paid her contributions into. Alarmed at this turn of events, Romand resolved to kill himself and his family. He went home, shot his wife and two children, and set the house on fire, only to be rescued at the last moment by firefighters. Sentenced to life imprisonment, he will be spending the rest of his days in an institution where the people looking after him are apparently impressed by his character and qualities.

The author says, quite rightly, that we do not in fact know who Romand really is. The impression we get is that he had somehow programmed himself to play the role of Dr. Romand for eighteen years and is now playing the role of the criminal Romand, displaying a degree of kindness that amazes the people around him.

Significantly, Carrère spends very little time describing the childhood of this man, although therein almost certainly lies the key to his strange behavior. All we are told is that the Romand family prided themselves on their honesty. But the boy never learned the truth about the things that were important to him. His mother had two miscarriages (or perhaps abortions), which distressed him, but he was not allowed to ask any questions about them. He was expected to conform to his parents' ideals, and so he did. He was an excellent student, never caused any problems, and lived up to his parents' expectations. But he had no idea who he was because he was forbidden everything that might have expressed his true self. We might be tempted to say that he was living a lie, but that would imply that he was conscious of what he was doing. My impression is rather that profound inner alienation was the only state he had ever experienced. Thus he was probably entirely unaware in his youth that he was playing a role.

When he decided to play the doctor a new element entered his life: conscious deception. He invested all his considerable ingenuity and energy into tricking others into giving him their love and affection and gradually milking them of their money in a way that they were completely powerless to see through. His conscious mind was fully preoccupied with this colossal ongoing hoax. But one thing had not changed: he could not allow himself to live out his own true feelings and needs. The loneliness of his early years persisted in the elaborate system of fabrications he had erected.

The real tragedy of people never given the chance to express their needs in childhood is that, without knowing it, they are leading a double life. As I made clear in *The Drama of the Gifted Child*, they have constructed a false self in childhood and do not know that they have another one where their suppressed feelings and needs are hidden away as effectively as if under lock and key. The reason for this is that they have never encountered anyone who could help them understand their distress, identify the prison in which their feelings are confined, break out of that confinement, and articulate their true feelings and genuine needs.

Romand is a spectacular instance of this phenomenon. Held in check for more than forty years, the truth finally found expression in the form of an appalling crime. There are countless other examples, perhaps less spectacular in their outcomes but in all cases destroying the lives of the people around them. The invariable aim of these people is to sustain the lie they have been upholding so as to gain the recognition or admiration they desperately need, which was denied them as children. In former times such people were labeled psychopaths; later the term sociopath gained currency; today they are termed narcissistic personalities or perverts. Whatever the term used to describe them, these people all have an inner void, a barrier denying them access to their true feelings.

Such people are often infinitely adaptable. Like chameleons they can adjust perfectly to their surroundings and when brought to justice are frequently model prisoners, as in the case of Romand. But even after the deed culminating in their imprisonment they still do not know who they really are. They go on playing the role that is expected of them in the given circumstances. First Romand was a loving father and husband, a true friend, an admired son and son-in-law. Then he wiped out his whole family and shortly afterwards became a prisoner liked and admired by all. But who is he really? No one knows—he himself probably least of all. To find that out, he would have had to stare into his own inner void, and it was precisely to avoid such an insight that he employed such amazing ingenuity for so many years.

The penal system does not address the questions posed by such cases, preferring to leave them to psychologists and psychiatrists. But psychologists and psychiatrists do not see it as their job to help these people find their true selves by confronting them with their childhoods. Instead they encourage them in their bids for total adjustment and hold this to be a sign of returning sanity.

I once heard a young, rather complacent warden say on television that in his prison the incestuous fathers all underwent group therapy where they learned to love their children, thus freeing themselves of the urge to abuse them. After the program I called him and asked whether many of those fathers had themselves been sexually abused in childhood. He answered that that was indeed "very frequently" the case, but that instead of snooping around in the past it was important to get them to see the adult responsibility they bore for their children in the here-and-now. This was his sincere conviction, and it is what the therapy groups were all about. I told him that in my view such an awareness of responsibility could be possible only after the men had discovered and mourned what had happened to them in childhood. I offered to send him a short paper I had written on the subject, but he declined. He left that kind of thing to the psychologists and psychiatrists, he said.

On television this man had presented an image of someone with progressive leanings, but he was not interested in hearing about the reasons why the men in his charge had wrecked their daughters' lives. For him the issue was a purely practical problem, to be solved with the same kind of approach as other matters of prison administration.

His response and his lack of interest were by no means surprising to me, but they were distressing because in this case a great deal is at stake. This young director was completely overlooking the fact that this was not merely a psychological but also a socioeconomic problem. A prisoner who finds out that he was sexually abused in his youth and who confronts the feelings that experience has left him with will very likely lose his compulsion to repeat the crime. I recently came across a newspaper article reporting on a study of three hundred serial killers in the United States, every one of whom had repeated their crimes after serving prison sentences, despite the therapy all had undergone. There is nothing surprising about that. If their therapy failed to search their childhoods for the motivations for the killings, then those causes will continue to fuel their destructive urges. Prison alone will not alter that fact. So if we can assume that exploratory therapy and encouragement to engage emotionally in uncovering childhood traumas can substantially shorten the actual term of imprisonment, then it is absurd to spend large amounts of taxpayers' money on immuring people in their own blindness and restricting their scope for new insights during their imprisonment. The split-off, denied, and repressed parts of their personalities can be reintegrated. Once that happens, there will be no more need to preach love and responsibility to them because they will see the necessity for themselves.

5

THE
SILENCE OF
THE CHURCH

———————————

*R*ELIGIOUS SCHOOLS of various denominations justify all forms of sadism by declaring them to be sanctioned by God or the prophets. Feminists have established that there is not one *sura* of the Koran that could qualify as support for the brutal custom of mutilating the genitals of young girls, though religious motives are trotted out in justification. Genital mutilation owes its existence solely to a male desire to exert total power over women and to the insistence of circumcised mothers and grandmothers on inflicting the same suffering on their daughters and granddaughters as they themselves experienced, while denying that there is any suffering involved.

The result is that today there are over 100 million women whose clitorises were removed at the age of ten, and most of them actively endorse this practice.

The government of the Federal Islamic Republic of the Comoros has announced its intention to introduce a ban on corporal punishment in order to defend—as its letter to the UN Committee on the Rights of the Child puts it—the right of children to a childhood free of torture. In contrast to the soft-pedaling encountered in most other bulletins on such questions, the letter makes surprisingly frank reference to the practices of Koranic schools, indicating in no uncertain terms the extent to which religion serves as a cover-up for the sadism of the teachers. For the pettiest offenses children are brutally flogged and otherwise humiliated beyond our worst imaginings. After the flogging they are tossed into a bathtub full of nettles or dragged half naked into the baking sunlight, where liquid sugar is poured over their bodies to attract insects that will torment them. Finally they are taken through the streets and forced to cry out their misdemeanors and do public penance for them.

Unlike some adult survivors of torture, children subjected to organized humiliation do not recount what has been done to them. They are too ashamed. Their conscious memories may in fact contrive to forget the torments or at least repress them. But their bodies have preserved every single detail, as their later behavior only too amply demon-

strates. These cruel punitive practices have been successfully represented to the children as righteous and proper,
and this is what will enable them to avenge themselves
without any qualms when they are old enough to do so.
Twenty years hence, some of these victims will themselves
become teachers at Koranic schools and inflict on their
charges and their own children the same treatment they
endured in childhood. And society will revere them for it
and commend them as God-fearing men going about their
sacred duties. Thus sadism is free to originate and flourish
under the cover of piety and religion. Those teachers were
not born sadistic; they learned to take pleasure in sadistic
practices at school and perhaps even earlier, at home. And
always with the injunction: This is for your own good!

As long as private Christian schools consider corporal
punishment for the children entrusted to their care to be
one of their religious duties, Christians condoning such
treatment have effectively forfeited any moral right to rail
against the practices at these Islamic schools. In the sum-
mer of 2000 the South African government, in the face of
vehement protest and resistance, introduced a ban on physical correction. On August 17, 2000, the government posted
a letter on the Internet from nearly two hundred Christian
groups demanding an exemption from this ban for the fourteen thousand young people in their care so that their in-
structors could "exercise their religious duties." Equally
blatant was their claim that teachers and parents have the

right to punish children. The pseudo-religious arguments notwithstanding, their sole concern—consciously or unconsciously—is to get even for the humiliations to which they themselves were once exposed by inflicting them on their own students. We can only hope the time will come when children will be taught that being beaten is a destructive act. If they can even be taught why this is so, eventually they will acquire an immunity to false information.

I receive letters from people all over the world telling me how much they suffered from the physical (and other) punishment dealt out to them at the Catholic boarding schools they attended. Conversely, some correspondents suggest that the situation has improved and that the Catholic church has long since abandoned its support of physical correction. Encouraged by this news, I addressed a letter to Pope John Paul II asking him to issue an appeal to parents-to-be that would open their eyes to the tragic consequences of beating their children. My conviction was that with this knowledge it would be easier for them to love their children and learn from them, rather than being misled by their own ignorance into turning their children into potential patients for physicians and psychotherapists who fail to understand the true meaning of the symptoms they display. I felt that an unequivocal plea from the pope, whose pronouncements are heeded by millions of Catholics worldwide, to refrain from beating children could have an immense impact.

As the latest psychological and neurological discoveries concerning child abuse are not yet widely known, and trusting that Pope John Paul would be moved by them, I did the best I could to outline those insights as briefly and cogently as possible. I had the letter translated into a number of different languages and made various attempts to ensure that it would be forwarded to the Holy Father personally. The reply I received makes me doubt this was the case.

The Vatican correspondent did not explicitly say that the pope had read the letter. He did reiterate that the church acknowledged the importance of child rearing and education and believed that children and young people must be treated "with patience and sensitivity if they are to achieve physical, mental, moral and spiritual maturity." My respondent also pointed out that the church had recently canonized an "outstanding and stalwart champion of young people," Father Marcellin Champagnat, the founder of the Marist Brothers, for his "great commitment to the cause of the young." The letter ended by extending a papal blessing to me and those "dear to me." Nowhere did this response from the Vatican refer to the important information and insights I had written about in my letter. Obviously the person I had asked to forward my letter and whose job it is to screen the mail was unable to relate to its contents. It is also conceivable that the information it contained aroused in them memories of their own upbringing, prompting them to dismiss my request out of hand. Not

only the Vatican itself but all the intermediary offices I
sent this letter to—in France, Switzerland, Poland, and the
United States—reacted in the same way. The only response
I received was the letter mentioned above, a formulaic reply without any bearing whatsoever on the concerns I had
expressed. A later attempt to interest Cardinal Jean-Marie
Lustiger, the archbishop of Paris, in the matter also failed.
My inquiry as to how I might best disseminate the latest
knowledge about the dangerous consequences of corporal
punishment received an evasive reply from the cardinal's
secretary. I was given to understand that the supreme
church authorities could not be expected to issue statements on "every problem" and that it was up to us layper-
sons to communicate our standpoint to others. One of the
questions I asked in my rejoinder to this was, "Is one to
conclude from your response that the principle of human
charity both preached and practiced by the church does not
extend to the sufferings of helpless children exposed to
physical violence?" (See my Web site, http://www.alice-
miller.com, for details of this correspondence in French
and German.)

I was of course not so naive as to suppose that a statement by the pope would suffice to change parents' behavior from one day to the next. But an acknowledgment of
the implications of this new information by an institution
that had tolerated and sometimes even advocated physical
correction for generations might in the long term have had

a major impact on the mentality of many believers. It usually takes a long time for scientific discoveries to filter down to the level of ordinary human reality and even longer to reach those who have had little schooling and who merely reenact the cruel treatment they received at the hands of their own parents. This attitude, tolerated as normal the world over, might have been radically altered by one single utterance from the pope. But it was not to be. For the present, at least, the church prefers to keep its silence on this point.

I do not know if my arguments will ever be able to reach the holy father. His biography tells us that his mother lavished loving care on him and that after her early death his father spent a great deal of time with him. But it is improbable that in his childhood he should have been completely spared the conventional view that it takes a strict upbringing to make boys into real men. Inextricably and tragically bound up with the love children feel for their parents, this conviction frequently asserts itself throughout a man's life. Challenging it may revive childhood anxieties. I can only hope that the pope will prove equal to this challenge once he appreciates that a few words from him would be sufficient to guard millions of children from the kind of abuse regularly administered to them.

Canonizing a nineteenth-century figure like Marcellin Champagnat for his alleged commitment to young people is not an adequate response to the enormous challenge of preventing violence and cruelty in this day and age. But this indication was all the Vatican saw fit to give me in reply to my appeal for intervention for the sake of children entrusted to its care.

Much the same response was accorded to Olivier Maurel when he attempted to expound the problem of corporal punishment for children to the bishops of France. I reproduce here his letter to the bishops' conference:

Your Excellency,

I take the liberty of approaching you because I am working on a book about corporal punishment of children. A host of recent research results show that physical correction, even in the apparently harmless form of smacks and slaps, can have severe consequences for the children. The United Nations Committee on the Rights of the Child has taken account of this fact and for ten years now has been regularly questioning the governments that have signed the UN Convention on the Rights of the Child. At five-year intervals, these countries are required to submit a report on the status of children's rights on their territory, with special reference to the use of physical force in families, schools, and the penal system. The reports and protocols of the Committee on the Rights of the Child in Geneva and the comments addressed to the respective states by that committee are accessible on the Web site http://www.unhchr.ch. In a frequently alarming way these texts all reveal that—albeit to various degrees—children all over the world are victims of what the report calls a veritable form of "xenophobia."

I would like to ask you what the Catholic Church is undertaking in this respect. The injunctions of the Gospels about the respect and protection to which children have a right could hardly be more unequivocal. How is this to be reconciled with an educational attitude where the humiliation of children is the rule rather than the exception? By their own admission, 80 percent of parents in France have recourse to physical violence as part of the child-rearing process. But my impression is that the Church has done nothing to speak out against such practices. Of course it has pilloried especially severe cases of child abuse, but the cases society elects to classify as such are exceptional instances where the perpetrators are conspicuous for their unusual cruelty and face legal prosecution for that reason. But the fact of the matter is that the distinctions between "child abuse," "parenting," and "disciplining" are entirely artificial. If the truth be told, children all over the world are exposed to physical blows administered in the name of the parents' right to bring up their children as they see fit.

In my attempt to collect reliable information on this point I have approached the editors of the journal *Missions africaines* because physical abuse is especially cruel and widespread on the African continent and the

Catholic Church is very strongly represented there. The reply from Father Claude Rémond was as follows: "Unfortunately I have no reliable sources on the degree to which the Church in Africa has been active in heightening parents' awareness of the problem of physical violence in child rearing." He kindly gave me the address of a nun in Togo who looks after street urchins. In her reply she confirmed the fact that child rearing in that area "cannot do without beating," adding that she did not have the impression that the Church was doing anything to counteract this attitude because sometimes she saw adults in church keeping order among the youth groups with sticks in their hands.

So where does the Catholic Church actually stand? Have there been any declarations by the Church on this problem? The pope and his bishops make frequent reference to the problem of violence in general. But to my knowledge they never make any mention of the fact that children have their first encounter with violence—slaps in the face, blows to the head, back, or buttocks—at the hands of those they love most, their parents. And this despite the fact that we now know that children learn not from what they are told but from the way they are treated. When adults are cruel it is because they, too, were once subjected to violence by those to whom they looked up. From earliest infancy they have had it drilled into them that conflicts can only be settled by brute force.

So what use is there in pillorying violence without making any reference to the sources it stems from?

I would be grateful if you could tell me whether there have been any official statements on this problem by the Church, the Pope, or the bishops. If you are unable to give me an answer, perhaps you would be so kind as to indicate to whom else I might address my inquiry.

Yours sincerely,
Olivier Maurel

Maurel appended to the copy of this letter he sent me the following note: "In reply, the secretariat of the French bishops' conference merely sent me a list of seven religious organizations allegedly concerned with these issues. I wrote to them all, but after two months the only reply I received informed me that the organization in question restricted its activities to torture perpetrated by governmental agencies."

Such persistent silence is alarming in the extreme. If this were not the first time the recipients had been informed of these findings, they would no doubt have indicated as much in their replies. But if it was the first time, then it is very hard to understand why they displayed such a lack of concern. Are we to believe that the welfare of future generations is a matter of supreme indifference to them? They themselves make frequent reference to the problem of violence and how it might be resolved. Surely we may assume that they are opposed to hatred and violence. Why, then, do they have no wish to know where that hatred comes from and how it evolves? Why do they choose to ignore the sources that have been pointed out to them?

What chance do we have of combating one of the most pernicious evils in society if we avert our gaze from it? The infantile fear of dealing with a painful topic makes us incapable of seeing the resources that we as adults can draw upon. We do have ways of preventing the constant reenactment of these evils. But in order to make use of them, we have to open our eyes.

If the Catholic church were to open its eyes, train its gaze on the cruelty being done to children, and speak out against it, would that have a detrimental effect on the power of the church? Probably, for at present that power rests squarely on the subjection of the faithful to its authoritarian decrees. If self-possessed believers were to begin questioning the power structures of the church, those structures would come tumbling down. Willful ignorance of the laws of psychology will, however, hardly suffice to preserve those structures.

But why does the church need this power in the first place? Is it not built around a principle of love and charity that should rule out concern for worldly power? And if so, why does it have so little faith in the power of love that it elects instead to cling to worldly power and demand unconditional obedience? Millions of people never ask them-

selves this question because they look to religion for protection and solace and believe that this is incompatible
with any kind of independent thinking. After the upbringing they have been through, they cannot imagine that God
could love people who had minds of their own and spoke
up for themselves. Like Adam and Eve, the price they have
paid for the love given them by their parents is unconditional obedience, blind faith, the voluntary renunciation of
knowledge and personal convictions—in short, the abandonment of their own true selves. They accept the authoritarian attitude of the church because it is something they
are only too familiar with from their own childhood: "We
know what you need better than you do. If you want to be
loved you must obey. You must never question our decisions. We are in no way accountable to the likes of you."

The spirit informing the story of Creation is obviously
the attitude by which such believers are guided. They wor-
ship in church, they meekly submit to the decrees issued
from above, and they never ask questions. Any inclinations
in that direction were radically drummed out of them as
children. But there is always the real danger that many of
them will be only too ready to place their obedience and
their followers' mentality at the service of other, much
more destructive taskmasters.

The diaries of Rudolf Höss, the commandant of
Auschwitz, point to the dangers of this kind of upbringing.
As a boy, Höss was remarkably well behaved and biddable,

browbeaten into following the wishes and injunctions of adults until the principles behind them became second nature to him. Today, people brought up like Höss display an astounding willingness to espouse the most abstruse ideologies of religious sects, neo-Nazi groups, or fundamentalist communities, and at the command of others (commands from others are indispensable!) will think nothing of destroying human lives and trampling on human dignity. They do not know that they are imitating the violation of their own dignity, which they were subjected to in childhood. The reason for their ignorance is that they were never allowed to become aware of that early humiliation for what it was. The principle of obedience was hammered home to them as a virtue, and they learned the lesson well. People who go through their entire childhood and youth with their fists clenched in their pockets will almost automatically use those fists as soon as someone tells them it is all right to do so.

How often does this spectacle have to repeat itself before churches and governments realize the drawbacks involved in unconditional obedience, before they are able to welcome a form of upbringing where children are encouraged to be critical and independent-minded, an upbringing where free-thinking children can feel loved and protected at home? Such children will feel no urge later in life to plant bombs, set fire to houses, and throw stones, and so will not have to go to prison for their deeds. Like Olivier

Maurel, I have addressed countless letters to high-ranking politicians, heads of state, prime ministers, and presidents, especially those of them who make frequent mention in their speeches of the alarming increase in juvenile violence. My aim has been to tell them precisely where that violence stems from, and that it is entirely within our power to do something to combat this escalation in the use of brute force once we have understood the sources it feeds on. But the response (or lack of it) was similar to the reaction that I got from the Vatican and that Maurel got from the bishops. The single answer I received came from the Ministry for Family Affairs of a major state thanking me for my interest in "childrearing" and completely ignoring the fact that I had written to them about *violence* in child rearing.

The vast majority of power holders in church and state are afraid of taking up the topic of violence in upbringing, either because they fear antagonizing voters and congregations or because they still feel the dread of retribution from their parents for unequivocally espousing the cause of the young child they once were. But if they believe that this would deprive them of their strength, then they are mistaken. On the contrary: their own history would support them if they could only resolve to face up to it and act in a consciously constructive way.

Evasive silence, abstention, willful ignorance, disregard for available information—all these attitudes may appear innocently passive. But they are tacit decisions that are bound to favor the destructive actions of young people because they immure them in the tradition of blind obedience, with all the dangerous consequences that tradition involves.

My personal experience with church authorities does not mean that there are not individual priests who appreciate the latest psychological findings. There are, and although they are certainly the exception at the moment, their activities may help lead to change for the better. One shining example is Donald Capps, professor of pastoral theology at Princeton Theological Seminary, who has never been afraid to draw on the sources of new insights about childhood and come up with his own exciting discoveries.

Capps's reflections on St. Augustine's destructive attitude toward his son show that one can remain a person of the church and still overcome emotional blindness. Millions of people regarded Augustine as a man of love because he wrote about the love of God. But Capps reveals him both as a severely beaten small child, who later glorified the practice of child beating (and wrote about children's innate badness), and as a father who rejected his only child ("born out of sin"). He regarded Augustine as a man who suppressed his own feelings and the strong authentic feelings of his son, and who probably caused his son's early death.

Capps's courageous discoveries may alarm some believers at first, but in the long run his insights may open their eyes to the circle of violence in their own hearts and help them free themselves from the tragic fate of their history. This fate was unavoidable for Augustine, but thanks to authors like Capps, today we can confront the truth and thus change our perspective.

6

BIOGRAPHICAL
BLIND SPOTS

---

*I*N THE PROLOGUE I talked about the history of Creation, my difficulties in accepting the image of a God who is both loving and vengeful and in believing arguments that seemed illogical. I should now like to present a different aspect of the Creation story. The forbidden fruit symbolizes for me not only abstract knowledge about good and evil but also, indeed mainly, the concrete knowledge we have of the beginnings of our own lives, knowledge that can show us very graphically how evil really comes about.

Like Adam and Eve before the Fall, we are born innocent. And like them, with shamefully few exceptions we are all confronted with commandments, threats, and punishment. Our parents project the repressed feelings of their own childhood onto us and without realizing it blame us for the things that once happened to them. Like the psychiatrist Henry in Brigitte's story (see Chapter 2), parents often react blindly and destructively because they are still caught up in the reality of their childhood without realizing it. To survive cruelties—beatings, humiliations, and neglect—they had to conceal their own feelings from themselves. Now they have become slaves to those emotions; they cannot control them because they cannot understand their meaning, and they cannot understand their meaning because, like Adam and Eve in Paradise, they have been told to regard cruelty as love. They have been taught to obey incomprehensible commandments and have been made to remain in a state of blindness all their lives, threatened with brimstone and hellfire should they dare to dissent.

Children are thus forbidden to see their parents' cruelty for what it is and are denied awareness of the cruelty they suffered in the earliest years of their lives. They are forced to believe that children feel no pain, that everything done to them was for their own good, and that if they suffered they only had themselves to blame—all this so that the deeds perpetrated by the parents can remain shrouded in darkness. But the body never forgets. As adults, they cannot simply rid themselves of what they knew as children. Though it may remain unconscious, that knowledge will dictate their behavior, will determine how they respond to

new experiences and ideas, and above all will influence relationships with their own children.

The forbidden fruit represents for me not only the injunction from outside but also the inner dictates of a young
organism. Small children cannot survive the truth; for
purely biological reasons they have no choice but to repress
what they know. But this repression, this refusal to recognize one's own origins, has a destructive effect. To offset
that effect we need enlightened witnesses—therapists,
counselors, and teachers who do not regard the emotions of
an adult as haphazard but see them as the logical fruits,
sometimes poisonous fruits, of a misguided process of in-
semination. With the help of knowledge, these will give
way to beneficial fruits that will not harm anyone. No one
has a natural propensity to feed on poisonous plants, but
some of us do that all the same because we know of no alternative, because we cling to what is familiar to us, those
things we have developed strategies to deal with, and
hence survive. If someone is present to help us recognize
the behavior patterns of our parents in the context of our
own childhoods, then we will no longer be forced to perpetuate those patterns blindly.

With the exception of psychohistorians, it is the rare biog-
rapher who delves into the childhood of political leaders, who
sometimes are in a position to make decisions that can mean
life or death for millions of people. In the thousands of books
about Hitler and Stalin hardly any mention is made of the

telltale details of their childhoods, and where mention is made, they are denied any crucial significance. There is much to learn by examining the biographies of two contrasting political leaders: Joseph Stalin and Mikhail Gorbachev.

Stalin was the only child of an alcoholic father who beat him soundly every day and a mother who never protected him, was herself beaten, and usually stayed away from home. Like Hitler's mother, she had already lost three children when her son was born. Joseph, the only surviving child, could never be sure that his father might not decide to kill him at the next opportunity. When he grew up, his suppressed panic was transformed into paranoia, the maniacal conviction that everyone was out to destroy him. In the 1930s, as absolute ruler of the Soviet Union, he had millions of people slaughtered or put into concentration camps. The impression one has is that this omnipotent and idolized dictator was in some way but a helpless child still fighting a hopeless battle against the overwhelming threat to his existence from a brutal father. In the trials orchestrated against free thinkers and so-called dissidents who were frequently his intellectual superiors, Stalin was perhaps trying to prevent his own father from killing the little boy he once was. Naturally he had no knowledge of this motive. If he had, it might have saved millions of lives.

A very different picture is presented by the Gorbachev family, which had no tradition of child beating but instead typically showed respect for children and their needs. As an adult, Mikhail Gorbachev has given ample evidence of qualities hardly any other living statesman has demonstrated to the same degree: the courage to look facts in the face and to seek flexible solutions, respect for others, give-and-take in the course of dialogue, absence of hypocrisy, and a complete lack of grandiosity in the conduct of his personal life. He has never been driven by blind self-assertion to make absurd decisions. Both his parents and his grandparents (the latter looked after him during the war years) appear to have been people with an unusual capacity for love and affection. The unanimous verdict on Gorbachev's father, who died in 1976, is that he was a lovable, modest man, amiable and peaceable in his dealings with others, a man who was never heard to raise his voice. The mother is described as sturdy, sincere, and cheerful. Even after her son had become a prominent public figure, she went on living modestly and happily in her small farmhouse. Gorbachev's childhood also supplies proof that poverty may have no adverse effect on the character of a child as long as that child's personal integrity is not damaged by hypocrisy, cruelty, abuse, corporal punishment, or psychological humiliation. Stalin's reign of terror, the horrors of war, the brutal occupation of his country, immense poverty, crippling physical labor—all these things Gorbachev lived through in his youth. But the emotional atmosphere prevailing at home afforded him protection and security.

One incident may serve as illustration. At the end of World War II Gorbachev, then a teenager, was unable to attend school for three months because he had no shoes to wear. When his father, in a field hospital recuperating from battle wounds, was told of this, he wrote to his wife that she must at all costs ensure that their son could go back to school because he was such an avid scholar. The mother sold the last of her sheep for fifteen hundred rubles in order to buy her son a pair of boots. His grandfather procured a warm coat for him and, at Mikhail's request, another one for a friend.

Protection and respect for the needs of a child—this is surely something we ought to be able to take for granted. But we live in a world full of people who have grown up deprived of their rights, deprived of respect. As adults they attempt to regain those rights by threat of force and violence. As Gorbachev's childhood is the exception rather than the rule, the society we live in continues to turn a blind eye to the facts of child abuse in all its forms. Among thousands of professors at hundreds of universities, there is not one single university chair for teaching about child abuse and cruelty to children. Why? Because that cruelty successfully masquerades as parenting and education.

When I bewail biographers' lack of interest in childhood, the frequent rejoinder is that for at least twenty years childhood has been a fashionable subject in literary works. In autobiographies many authors dwell on their childhood years. Also, there is less of a tendency today to idealize and romanticize childhood; the misery frequently comes across in all its starkness. But in most autobiographies I have read the authors still maintain an emotional distance from the suffering they went through as children. Little empathy and an astounding absence of rebellion are the rule. There is no inquiry into the whys and wherefores behind the injustice, the emotional blindness and the resulting cruelty displayed by the adults, whether teachers or parents. Description is all. On every page of the brilliant book *Angela's Ashes*, for example, Frank McCourt describes such cruelties in gruesome detail. But even as he recalls his childhood, he never rises up against his tormentors, attempting instead to remain loving and tolerance and seeking salvation in humor. And it is for this humor that he has been celebrated by millions of readers the world over.

But how are we to stand up for children in our society and improve their situation if we laugh at and tolerate cruelty, arrogance, and dangerous stupidity? An extract from McCourt's book illustrates his attitude:

There are seven masters in Leamy's National School and they all have leather straps, canes, blackthorn sticks. . . .

They hit you if you can't say your name in Irish, if you can't say the Hail Mary in Irish, if you can't ask for the lavatory pass in Irish.

It helps to listen to the big boys ahead of you. They can tell you about the master you have now, what he likes and what he hates.

One master will hit you if you don't know that Eamon De Valera is the greatest man that ever lived. Another master will hit you if you don't know that Michael Collins was the greatest man that ever lived.

Mr. Benson hates America and you have to remember to hate America or he'll hit you.

Mr. O'Dea hates England and you have to remember to hate England or he'll hit you.

If you ever say anything good about Oliver Cromwell they'll all hit you.

Humor saved Frank McCourt's life and enabled him to write his book. His readers are grateful to him for it. Many of them have shared the same fate and they want nothing more dearly than to be able to laugh it off. Laughter is good for you, so they say, and it certainly helps you survive. But laughter can also entice you to be blind. You may be able to laugh at the fact that someone has forbidden you to eat of the tree of knowledge, but that laughter will not really wake you up from your sleep. You must learn to understand the difference between good and evil if you want to understand yourself and change anything in the world as it is.

Laughter is good for you, but only when there is reason to laugh. Laughing away one's own suffering is a form of fending off pain, a response that can prevent us from see-ing and tapping the sources of understanding around us.

If biographers were better informed about the details and consequences of what some indifferently call a normal strict upbringing, they could provide us with precious ma-terial for better understanding our world. But there are not many who try to figure out how such upbringing was ex-perienced by their subject as a child.

Part II

HOW
WE ARE STRUCK
EMOTIONALLY
BLIND

ℛECENTLY I WAS sent an exchange of letters addressed in July 2000 to the Project NoSpank Web site. I quote it here in full because in it a father indicates in the space of a few paragraphs something I shall be attempting to explain at greater length in Chapter 7. Though this father does not appear to be aware of precisely what he is describing, he is at least on the right track.

Hello,

First let me say that I find your site very informative. I was a believer in paddling because when I grew up I was paddled. My father was a school principal and paddled many students. I felt it did no serious damage until the birth of my son. My wife was potty training him when he was three years old and he got off the potty and she spanked him very hard on his bare bottom. He immediately began to cry and it made my stomach turn. I became enraged!! She spanks the children regularly and says she was paddled several times in school when she was a child. It seems like there is something more that happened to her when she was paddled in school but she refuses to talk about it.

Is there any way you know of to find out exactly what happened back then circa 1965–1975 when she was paddled? Would there be any public record of this and if so how can we get this information? Would the school district or the school itself have any record of this? Any help would be greatly appreciated. She was paddled on three separate occasions in Warren, Ohio, in the Warren City School District while attending Harry B. Turner Middle School. I don't know if you can help but anything at all would be great.

Thank you very much, keep up the good work,

C.S.

Dear C.S.

My advice is for you not to spend precious time attempting to discover something in the records of your wife's old school. If, by some miracle, a record of what you are looking for had been preserved, the district would never let you lay your hands on it. And even if you learned what happened to her as a schoolgirl, what use could you make of that information? Your wife apparently is intent on avoiding those memories, and is busy restaging her childhood traumas on her own children. I can understand your interest in digging into family history for the purpose of uncovering clues that might explain current behavior, but wouldn't it be wiser to do that later, after you've protected your children? This is not the kind of business one can postpone. You wouldn't want your children to wonder years hence what the rational parent was busy with when they urgently needed an ally. The very next letter . . . supports my sense of urgency in this matter, and seems to hold a message for you. . . . Please read it. That said, I will post this correspondence on Project NoSpank (without your name, of course) and if anyone responds with information about paddling practices at your wife's old school during the period you mentioned, I'll forward it to you.

Jordan

The letter Jordan is referring to runs as follows:

As a child, I was so severely spanked that I would lose all control over my bowels and bladder, and defecated all over myself, still the beating would go on, spreading the mess to cover large parts of my body. I don't know if my mother was in another room, or outside of the home, just know that she was not defending me, verbally or physically. The humiliation of having to clean myself up, change clothes, while crying was so deeply buried, until I read this "Plain Talk about Spanking."

Thank you. Please do not use my name.

The author of the first letter is upset that his wife constantly spanks their children. He intuits that there must be some connection between what he has seen and something that happened to his wife when she was a schoolgirl. He sets out to investigate and envisages inquiring into the matter with the school authorities. By doing so he is in fact withdrawing from his emotions rather than being guided by them. It is probable that his wife was beaten not only at school but much earlier, which is why she uses the same methods on her children.

But how did the letter writer feel about the beatings he himself received as a child from his father, a school principal portrayed as something of a professional spanker? The question is not explicitly addressed in the letter. To be able to ask it, the son would have needed an enlightened witness to help him to experience the small boy's fear, to face up to the pain, and to take his bearings from those memories the next time he is overcome by rage.

What is the significance of that rage today? To whom is it directed? The letter gives us no clue. Is the father on his children's side and angry at his wife, or is it the children's reactions that arouse his rage by reminding him of the pain he once had to suppress? He feels that something else must have happened in his wife's childhood because up to now he has considered spanking alone to be normal and harmless, even advocating it himself for a long time. But now that he has discovered the NoSpank Web site, he appears to want more information.

This story suggests that emotional blindness can be overcome, a process I will discuss in the following chapter.

7

BARRIERS

IN THE MIND

---

*R*EADERS FREQUENTLY tell me of the hostility they encounter when they declare their allegiance to the cause of protecting children. Their attitude challenges a system that for most people represents a familiar, reassuring frame of reference. New information can be a source of uncertainty, and in the face of uncertainty the temptation is to resort to threatening behavior—similar to the intimidation parents use to bring their children up to be "good" and always do as they are told. This confronts enlightened witnesses with the same kind of painful rejection that children experience at the hands of their parents.

In some cases the reaction is so extreme that it amounts to moral condemnation, if not downright ostracism. It bears similarities to the hatred that led to the systematic persecution of the early Christians. Though the effects of this hatred are by no means comparable (the early Christians were brutally tortured and slain), there are significant parallels between the fury aroused in both cases by people openly supporting the protection of children that was preached and practiced by Jesus himself ("Suffer the little children to come unto me," Mark 10:14).

When the church was able to establish temporal power, the persecution of Christians came to an end. The champions of children do not need the assistance of a powerful institution like the church in order to resist the hostile pressure against them. Their strength lies in their knowledge of the laws governing childhood and indeed life itself, laws that can be objectively verified. Some of the most important testimonies we have in this respect are the reports of people who suffered abuse in childhood, which reveal the dire consequences such cruelty has on the way they treat their own children. This truth cannot be destroyed. Each day it receives more and more confirmation.

Recently brain research has been furnishing additional proof. The brain of a child is not yet fully formed at birth but develops its final structure over the first three years of life. Under certain circumstances the messages the brain receives in those formative years may imprint themselves more indelibly than any other information it will ever be required to process. The sensations and instructions coming from the mother or other important figures can live on for decades. And although we never hear anyone suggest that children should be humiliated, derided, or deceived, we do hear that spanking is good for them. Many of us were told this ourselves when we were small, as a perverse accompaniment to the slaps and beatings to which we were subjected. (See the forum on my Web site.)

A number of researchers have established that neglect and traumatization of baby animals invariably leads to both functional and structural deficiencies in their brains. Gradually this effect is being found to be true for human babies as well. The profound implications of these findings are alarming. Many parents who never received love and care when they were small, who were trained to be obedient above all else, may, with the best of intentions, have done the same to their children. They are likely to find this new information highly unsettling, if not unbearable. I can therefore understand why scientists are reluctant to spell out their findings in unequivocal terms. Instead of saying, "We have found that what applies to animals also applies to humans," they tend to say, "Maltreatment *may* lead to lesions and deficiencies in the structure of the brain." This strategy not only helps their findings get accepted but also protects them from the charge of being unscientific. Their equivocation, however, encourages denial and self-deception. Much as inveterate smokers say things like, "My grandfather smoked all his life but never got cancer, and he was over eighty when he died," many people hearing of the new brain research may say, "I was beaten as a child and I turned out perfectly fine. If scientists say spanking may lead to brain damage, they're also saying that it may not." These people have no inkling of how they might have turned out if they had not been spanked. Any impairments resulting from the abuse are outside the range of their awareness, just as a person without empathy does not know what empathy means.

When I read of the recent progress in brain research and the results of the work being done on early infancy, it helped me to realize why the effects of those first lessons and messages are so persistent. Armed with this new information, I would say to mothers today: "Don't be distressed if you find yourselves involuntarily giving your children a smack. It's something your hand learned very early on; it happens almost automatically, and you can usually limit the damage by recognizing that you made a mistake and admitting your error. But whatever you do, don't ever tell your children you hit them for their own good. If you do, you will be contributing to the perpetuation of willful stupidity and covert sadism."

Modern brain research has confirmed the structure of repression, denial, and splitting off which I proposed in my 1981 book *Thou Shalt Not Be Aware* to describe the processes our emotions are subjected to in early childhood. Many authors have indicated how important an early attachment to a key person is in order for a child's intelli-

gence to develop normally. Daniel Goleman makes contin-
ued reference to "emotional intelligence," but Katharina
Zimmer and others have shown that the development of
the intelligence *as such* is inextricably linked with the
emotions experienced in early childhood.

This explains why the necessity of repressing pain in
childhood leads not only to the denial of one's personal history but also to a denial of the suffering of children in general, and thus to major deficits in our cognitive capacity.
This desensitization finds expression in the use of corporal
punishment in educational settings and in the practice of
circumcision (for both sexes). I am deeply convinced that
the absence of a good relationship with the mother or some
mother substitute, coupled with physical abuse, including
the kind of corporal punishment meted out in the name of
good parenting, is among the sources that give rise to this
lack of sensitivity and the barriers in the mind.

The work of leading brain specialists such as Joseph
LeDoux, Debra Niehoff, Candace Pert, Daniel Schacter,
and Robert Sapolsky demonstrates that very early deficits
in a child's communication with a primary caregiver can
lead to defects in the brain. Small children who are beaten
or otherwise abused also display such damage because, as
we saw earlier, a condition of extreme stress can bring
about the destruction of newly formed neurons and their
interconnections. (The same thing can happen, inciden-
tally, when a fetus is exposed to extreme overstimulation—

for example, hours and hours of recorded music "in order to produce a Mozart at birth," as one Spanish manual for parents recommends. For a child's brain to develop freely it needs stimulation geared to its own specific rhythms, not enforced stimulation from outside.) The consensus is that early emotions leave indelible traces in the body and are encoded as information that will have a serious impact on the way we feel and think as adults, although those effects normally remain beyond the reach of the conscious mind and logical thought.

These discoveries provide an essential key to understanding this whole issue, albeit one that, as far as I know, scientists have yet to make use of. Occasionally—for example, in Candace Pert's exciting account of the discovery of the emotion molecule—one has the impression that, helpful as such experiments are in producing more and more new keys, there appears to be little interest in finding the locks they might fit.

One of the great exceptions is Joseph LeDoux, who at the close of his book *The Emotional Brain* postulates a form of collaboration between the cognitive and the emotional systems. Though his remarks clearly reflect the power and persistence of early emotional (corporal) memories and the frequent inability of our conscious minds to come to grips with the powerful and lasting impact they have, LeDoux insists that such a collaboration is absolutely necessary. But he is not a therapist, and he limits himself

to the statements he can responsibly make as a brain re-
searcher, conceding openly that he does not know how a
bridge might be built between the emotional knowledge of
the body (the unconscious) and its cognitive faculties. From
my own self-experience and from my experience with others, I know that this does take place in therapies systematically addressing the traumatic experiences and emotions
of childhood and thus weakening those barriers in our
minds. Once this has happened it is possible to activate areas of the brain not hitherto drawn upon, presumably for
fear of the pain and distress that recalling early instances
of abuse would arouse.

This emotional learning process can take considerable
time, and an enlightened witness is indispensable if it is to
succeed. For decades I was convinced I had never been
beaten as a child because I had no conscious memory of it.
But reading through the advice given by poisonous pedagogy I learned that in the period of my birth children were
beaten very early, sometimes in the first few months of
their lives, in order to train them to obey and to use the toi-
let, and it was then that I realized why I had no recall. I
had been so effectively taught to obey when I was still a
baby that the only memories I have of this chastisement
are implicit body memories as opposed to explicit conscious memories. Later, my mother proudly told me that I
was fully toilet-trained by the age of six months and never
caused any trouble—except when I insisted on having my

own way. Then all that was needed was a stern look from her and I soon came to my senses. Today I know the high price I paid. The fear of that stern look stopped me from saying, or even so much as thinking, what I wanted. But I finally did achieve that ability.

It is a never-ending source of acute distress for me when I think of the devastating power of denial in producing the barriers in our minds. One of the ways this obstructive power manifests itself is in the persistence of theologians and philosophers in discussing ethical issues without taking any account of the findings produced by brain research and the laws governing infant development. These factors are crucial to a clearer understanding of how evil originates and how we actively perpetuate it. For psychoanalysts it is also high time to rethink the concepts of destructive drives and evil, "perverted" children, which they have inherited from poisonous pedagogy. But in order to do so they would have to take modern research on infancy seriously. The approach adopted by Daniel Stern and the followers of John Bowlby still appears to gain only peripheral attention in psychoanalytic circles, perhaps because by his theory of initial attachment Bowlby exploded a taboo. By linking the causes of antisocial behavior with the absence of a resilient attachment to the mother, he was flying in the face of Freud's drive theory.

But my conviction is that we have to go a step further than Bowlby went. We are dealing here not just with antisocial behavior and so-called narcissistic disorders but with the inescapable realization that denying and repressing our childhood traumas means reducing our capacity to think and conspiring to erect barriers in our minds. Brain research has succeeded in uncovering the biological foundations of the denial phenomenon. But the consequences, the impact on our mentality, have not yet been adequately contemplated. No one appears to be interested in examining how insensitivity to the suffering of children—a phenomenon found the world over—is bound up with *a form of mental paralysis that has its roots in childhood.*

As children, we learn to suppress and deny natural feelings and to believe sincerely that the cuffs and blows we receive are for our own good and do us no lasting injury. Our brains, furnished with this false information, then instruct us to raise our own children by the same methods, telling them that it is good for them just as it was good for us.

This way of thinking causes billions of people to believe that children can become good and decent citizens only if we do violence to them. They are blind to the fear in their children's eyes and refuse to acknowledge that the only thing we can really instill in children by beating them is the determination to use violence later in life, either against themselves or against others. These destructive beliefs, also held by many intellectuals, are impervious to argument because they are stored in the body at a very early stage. Such people will make blunt assertions that, without their realizing it, stand in the starkest contrast to the pure intellectual knowledge they acquired from books.

During one of my workshops a psychology professor said, "In general I'm in agreement with you, but I cannot endorse your efforts to get corporal punishment legally banned because it deprives parents of a way of instilling certain values in their children, and I find that important. My children are three and five, and they've got to learn what they're allowed to do and what they aren't. If a law like that really got passed, it might stop many young people from having children at all."

I asked the man whether he had been beaten in childhood. He said yes, but only when it was necessary, when he had really driven his father to it, and then he had regarded the punishment as fair. I asked him how old he was when he was beaten for the last time and he said he was seventeen; his father had been beside himself with rage over some bit of teenage mischief. When I asked him for details, after a brief silence the man said, "I can't remember. It's all such a long time ago, but it must have been something serious because I can remember how my father's face was twisted into a grimace. My father was very fair, so I must have deserved the punishment."

I was stunned. This man, who taught developmental psychology, who had committed himself to the cause of abolishing cruelty to children, still refused to see anything wrong with corporal punishment as part of parenting. The barrier in his mind revealed itself bluntly. There must have been reasons for it, I thought, probably buried in early anxiety. I hesitated for a moment, then decided that those reasons needed to be dragged to the surface.

I confronted him. "You say you were seventeen at the time and you can't remember what you'd done—all you can remember is your father's face twisted into a grimace. From that you conclude that your punishment must have been deserved. But you expect your three- and five-year-old children to internalize the well-meaning principles you try to impress on them when you spank them. What makes you think that a small child is better able to understand these lessons and get some good out of them than you were as an adolescent? All a beaten child remembers is fear and the faces of the angry parents, not why the beating was taking place. Like you, the child will assume he had been naughty and merited the punishment. What kind of beneficial pedagogical effect do you see in that?"

I received no answer to my questions, but the next day the man said that he had had a sleepless night and needed to think things over. I was pleased by this response because it meant that there was something going on in his mind. Most people fear this kind of opening up. They merely rehearse their parents' opinions without realizing that they are floundering in logical contradictions because as children they learned not to feel their own pain.

But the embers of that pain are not extinguished. If they were, we would not feel compelled to go on doing to others what was done to us when we were small. The memory traces we believe to have been blotted out forever persist and are still operative. This realization sinks in when we become aware of our own behavior.

I never cease to be amazed by the precision with which people often reproduce their parents' behavior, although they have no memory of their own early childhoods. A father will beat his son and humiliate him with sarcastic remarks but not have any memory whatsoever of having been similarly humiliated by his own father. Only in a searching therapeutic context will he (ideally) recall what happened to him at the same age. Merely forgetting early traumas and early neglect is no solution. The past always catches up with us, in our relationships with other people and especially with our children.

What can we do about this? We can try to become aware of what we ourselves suffered, of the beliefs we adopted in childhood as gospel truth, and then confront these beliefs with what we know today. This will help us to see and feel things to which we have closed our minds, for in the absence of a witness who can empathize with us and genuinely listen to us, we have no other way of protecting ourselves from the searing force of the pain. With the help of an enlightened witness, our early emotions will stand revealed, take on meaning for us, and hence be available for us to work on.

But without such empathy, without any understanding of the context of a traumatic childhood, our emotions will remain in a chaotic state and will continue to cause us profound, instinctive alarm. By recourse to ideologies of all kinds, we manage to muffle this alarm so effectively that its true origins remain completely obscured.

In the Preface I made brief reference to the origins of barriers in the mind and the way they function. It is now time to illustrate those mechanisms in greater detail. On the one hand, barriers in the mind are our friends because they protect us from pain and enable us to fend off the anxieties aroused by events in our past. On the other hand, this same action makes barriers our enemies, as they cause emotional blindness and urge us to do harm to ourselves and others.

In a bid to blot out the fear and pain of our abused younger self, we erase what we know can help us, fall prey to the seductiveness of sects and cults, fail to see through all kinds of lies, and assert that children need physical "correction." In this chapter my aim is to supply not an abstract discussion of barriers in the mind but concrete examples with which you may be able to identify. As every childhood history is fundamentally unique (despite certain shared elements, such as humiliation and insensitivity to suffering), the denied and split-off components are not the same in all cases. Though millions may be prompted by their own tragic histories and their emotional blindness to elect charlatans or even psychopaths as their leaders, there will always be some people in every country who were not abused in childhood or who had the benefit of helping witnesses. As adults they will be able to see through fabrications and assess real dangers. This may be the best chance we have for progress and democracy.

Emotional blindness can be well studied by examining the careers of sect members. Jehovah's Witnesses, for example, are in favor of corporal punishment and constantly warn that the end of the world is near. They are not aware that they bear within themselves the abused children they once were, and that they already experienced the end of the world when their loving parents beat them. What could be worse than that? But the Jehovah's Witnesses learned very early not to recall their pain and to tell their children that hitting doesn't hurt. The reality of the end of the world is constantly on their minds, but they do not know why.

The Romanian dictator Nicolae Ceausescu knew nothing of the way he had suffered as a child from having been pent up in one room with ten brothers and sisters in a state of extreme neglect. As an adult living in the monomaniacal opulence of luxurious palaces he repressed all explicit memory of it. But implicit (body) memories of his childhood sufferings remained, and they incited him to take vengeance on a whole nation. Like his own mother, the women in his dictatorship were not allowed to have abortions. Like his own parents, most couples in Romania were forced to have more children than they wanted or were able to care for. As a result Romanian orphanages were full to bursting with youngsters displaying severe behavioral disorders and disabilities caused by extreme neglect. Who needed all those children? No one. Only the dictator himself, whose unconscious memories spurred him to commit atrocities and whose mental barriers prevented him from recognizing them as atrocities.

Many of my critics protest that one cannot trace world events back to the childhood of a single person. But I have never asserted that the causes I have discovered are the only ones conditioning the course of history. What I do keep pointing out is the consistency with which they have been ignored. I stand accused of using arguments that I have never put forward. Extreme simplifications of my stance can be found in books by the British historian Ian Kershaw, whose exemplary thoroughness in researching Hitler's life lends the appearance of accuracy. Unfortunately, he simply does not have the personal and conscious experience with the emotional world of children that would enable him to understand his subject more acutely.

Kershaw appears to have no awareness of this process of discharging infant emotions in adult life, nor of their transformation into destructive hatred. The barriers in his mind allow him to study thousands of details in Hitler's life while ignoring the question "Why Hitler?" the answer to which is locked away in the dictator's childhood.

This question is posed immediately in the title of the French translation of Ron Rosenbaum's book on Hitler, *Pourquoi Hitler?*, but Rosenbaum does not answer it. (The title of the U.S. edition is *Explaining Hitler.*) He is content to offer a journalistic compilation of data and anecdotes without reflection. He, too, is at pains to respect the taboo and divert his gaze from the place that holds the key, although he had access to such insightful studies of Hitler as those by Robert G. L. Waite, whom he quotes in his book.

Pointing to the barriers erected in our minds in early childhood is not a psychoanalytic interpretation but a statement that can be tested and verified for each individual. But value judgments may insinuate themselves into the testing and thus distort the picture. Every criminal was humiliated, neglected, or abused in childhood, but few of them can admit to it. Many genuinely do not know that they were. Thus denial gets in the way of statistical surveys based on the question-and-answer method, none of which will have any practical prophylactic effect as long as our eyes and ears remain closed to the issues posed by childhood.

We do have concrete scientific evidence for some issues, though. We know, for instance, that children who have been beaten and "corrected" are more obedient in the short term but more aggressive and destructive in the long term. Unfortunately, what psychologists have laboriously assembled and proved can be flouted in the media. In May 2000 the *Wall Street Journal* published an article titled "Spanking Comes Back" that revealed new research findings allegedly indicating that today's young parents are prone to beat their children even if they themselves were not maltreated in childhood. But we normally do not have any conscious memory of the smacks and spanking we received in early infancy. So statements such as "I was never beaten" are not reliable. My own exhaustive research on this topic has established that only people beaten in childhood feel the compulsion to beat their own children (which does not mean that they necessarily give in to the urge). People who were never beaten may also have difficulties with their children but do not feel compelled to hit them because their bodies have not stored the corresponding memories.

Science has no major impact on the way children are raised. The power for change will not come from the universities but rather from courageous individuals—lawyers, judges, politicians, nurses, midwives, and enlightened parents and teachers committed to putting nonviolent education and parenting on a firm legislative footing. The campaign initiated by Marilyn Fayre Milos, co-founder and director of the National Organization of Circumcision Information Resource Centers (NOCIRC), to stop routine circumcision in American hospitals was initially supported by only a few other nurses. But their refusal to assist in this cruel procedure quickly enlisted public support as people realized that they had been uncritically accepting its arbitrary practice. These operations now require the consent of the parents before they can be performed.

What was it that stopped male doctors from inflicting unnecessary suffering on a newborn child? Why were they blind for so long to the fact that they were abusing a defenseless victim? Simply because they were themselves the victims of such maltreatment in their own infancy and had internalized the message that it was painless and harmless. Thanks to the initiative of one nurse, many people are now aware that a small child will suffer physical and psychological harm from such interference. Only a few years ago the operations were performed without anesthesia. Here we are in the presence not only of a lack of compassion but of formidable barriers in the mind. How else could so many have believed that adults undergoing an operation must be given anesthesia to block the pain but highly sensitive newborns do not require similar assistance? Such brutal procedures are bound to cause the kind of thought paralysis we have been examining. It was not male doctors who put an end to the destructive custom of routine circumcision but female nurses, who had not undergone such treatment themselves.

The new law passed by the German parliament in July 2000 prohibiting corporal punishment is another decisive step toward the humanization of our personal relations and the removal of barriers in the mind. Significantly, it owes its existence to politicians and lawyers, most of them women. Psychotherapists and psychologists (male and female) have been notably less committed in this respect, although they are confronted every day with the consequences of childhood traumas. Twenty years ago Sweden's therapists actually campaigned against such an initiative, contending that a ban would so antagonize parents that they would take it out on their children in other ways. As I demonstrated in *The Drama of the Gifted Child*, the career of a psychologist begins in childhood with the desperate attempt to understand the parents without judging them. We should not remain bogged down in the fears of our childhood. As adults we must summon up the courage to judge, to call evil by its name and not tolerate it.

The much-needed change in our mentality will take place in stages. Children today who are never beaten will think and feel differently in twenty years from the way we think and feel today. This is my firm conviction. They will have eyes and ears for the suffering of their own children, and this will do more to effect change than statistical surveys ever could. My optimism is based on the principle of prevention, of forestalling violence in childhood by means of legislation and parent education.

I am often asked what we can do to help those people already seriously harmed by the processes I have been describing. Do they all have to undergo lengthy courses of therapy? The quality of therapy has nothing to do with the time it takes. I know people who have spent decades going to psychoanalysts and are still ignorant of what went on in their childhood because the analysts themselves are reluctant to venture onto that terrain in search of their own childhood realities. For some years now, new directions in therapy targeted at traumas of this kind have frequently achieved success in a short space of time. One of them is Eye Movement Desensitization and Reprocessing (EMDR), developed by Francine Shapiro. I have too little experience of these therapies to understand why they are effective, but I can imagine that in many cases the therapist's interest in the traumatic experiences is enough to initiate a process whereby the language of the body is accorded the significance it merits. In classical psychoanalysis, centered on the interpretation of fantasies, this process is not one of the objectives. I myself have been through three classical analyses, all with well-intentioned analysts, but none of them helped me dig down to the reality of my early childhood.

I tried next to get on the track of it with the help of primal therapy. I succeeded in discovering many of the feelings I had had in early infancy but failed to understand the entire context of early childhood reality and to allow the truth to surface because I had no enlightened witness to stand by me in this endeavor. Today I would not readily ad-

vise anyone to pursue this course (unless they are very certain of the therapist's qualifications and expertise) because
many apparently enlightened witnesses may arouse intense feelings in their patients without assisting them in
extricating themselves from their personal chaos.

I am frequently asked what I consider to be the decisive
factor in psychotherapy today. Is it, as I have attempted to
show in this book, the emotional and cognitive recognition
of the truth, liberation from the enforced vow of silence
and from idealization of one's parents? Or is it the presence
of an enlightened witness? My view is that it is not a question of either-or but of both-and. Without an enlightened
witness it is impossible to bear the truth of what happened
to us in early infancy. But by the term *enlightened witness*
I do not mean anyone who has studied psychology or has
been through primal experiences with a guru and remained in his thrall. For me, enlightened witnesses are
therapists with the courage to face up to their own histories and thereby to gain their autonomy rather than seeking to offset their own repressed feelings of ineffectuality
by exercising power over their patients.

In the story of the psychiatrist Henry, told in Chapter 2,
I was attempting to convey how it might have been possible to give him more help with a different therapeutic de-
sign. In theoretical terms, Henry needs to be able to identify all those points in everyday life where traces of his
infant reality rise to the surface, to learn to recognize them

for what they are and not to act out blindly. He needs assistance in coping emotionally with present situations as an adult while at the same time maintaining contact with the suffering and knowing child he once was, the child he could not muster the courage to listen to for so long but now, with help, can finally heed.

The body knows everything that has happened to it, but it has no language to express that knowledge. It is like the children we once were, the children who see all but, without the aid of the adults, remain helpless and alone. Accordingly, whenever the emotions from the past rise to the surface they are invariably accompanied by the fears of the helpless child dependent on the understanding, or at least the reassurances, of the parents. Even parents at a loss to understand their children because they are unaware of their own histories can provide such reassurance. They can assuage the children's fears (and their own) by giving them protection, safety, and continuity. And our cognitive system, in dialogue with the body, can do the same.

Unlike the body, our cognitive system knows little of the events in the distant past, for conscious memories are fragmentary, brittle, unreliable. But it has a huge fund of knowledge at its disposal, the faculties of a fully developed mind, and the life experiences a child cannot yet have. As adults are no longer powerless, they can offer the child within them (the body) protection and an attentive ear so that it can express itself in its own way and tell its story. In the light of these stories, the looming, incomprehensible fears and emotions of the adult take on meaning. Finally they stand in a recognizable context, no longer obscurely menacing.

Early anxieties stored in the body can be resolved in therapy as long as their causes are not denied. Initial moves toward a therapeutic concept of this kind have been with us for a number of years now, frequently in the form of counseling for self-therapy, counseling of a kind that I once advocated myself. I no longer recommend this course. I feel strongly that we need the company of an enlightened witness to embark on the journey. Unfortunately, it is rare for therapists to have enjoyed such company in their own training. I am only too well aware of the various forms of anxiety assailing therapists, their fear of hurting their parents if they dare to face their own childhood distress head on and without embellishment, and the resultant reluctance to support their patients fully in their search. But the more we write and talk on the subject, the sooner this state of affairs will change and the anxieties lose some of their power over us. In a society with a receptive attitude toward the distress of children, none of us will be alone with our histories. Therapists will be more inclined to forsake Freud's principle of neutrality and to take the side of the children their clients once were. This will give those clients the perspective they need to confront their own histories.

Part III

BREAKING THROUGH: DISCOVERING OUR CHILDHOOD HISTORIES

*U*P TO THIS point my concern has been to show that society still treats the subject of childhood reality as taboo and to explain why. In the remainder of the book I ask what we can do as individuals to free ourselves of the commandment "Thou shalt not be aware" and proceed from there to the realization "That's how it was" and finally to resolve, "I'm going to treat my children differently."

I know many different kinds of people who have taken this step, and in the following chapters I describe their awakenings. I turn first to young people who, thanks to their new insights, have regained their empathy for the sensitive natures of children before becoming parents themselves. Then I give an account of young mothers who, encouraged by the close physical relationship in breast-feeding their babies, recognize the traces of the cruelties they experienced in childhood and protect their children from a blind acting-out of their emotions. In my subsequent description of the analyst Harry Guntrip I am con-

cerned with the resurfacing of things repressed following
the birth of a person's first child.

I end with the story of a woman who tried all her life to
do the right thing and constantly suppressed her own feelings and perceptions because she had been taught very
early to ignore them and to obey and conform at all costs.
This enforced overadjustment later became a part of the
core of her personality and prompted her to persist in trying to make cripplingly unsatisfactory personal relationships work. Only when she developed a life-threatening
illness was she able to see through and consequently abandon the strategy of unconditional obedience that dated
back to her infancy, discover her own needs, and understand that she invariably attempted to assert those needs in
situations where it was impossible to fulfill them. She had
spent decades recapitulating the distress she went through
in her childhood when the fulfillment of those needs was
out of the question. Her fatal illness brought her into contact with an enlightened witness, and with the help of that
person she finally realized that there was no necessity for
the distress of her childhood to persist in her adult life and
that she was no longer powerless to prevent it.

As a child, she had been dependent on her parents. As an
adult, she was free to mix with people who shared her conscious desire for communication. She did not have to force
her unconscious needs onto people who had no desire for
the kind of communication she was looking for.

Could this woman have taken that step without therapy? There is no unequivocal answer. Many people, indeed, manage to abandon their projections and extricate themselves from destructive relationships without professional help. Others, however, cannot achieve such liberation even with the aid of therapy because they are unable to reach down to the childhood roots of their overadjustment.

Each of us must decide for ourselves what risks we are prepared to take and what digging deep into our past really means to us.

8

TALKING

IT THROUGH

---

*E*VER SINCE I became aware that hitting children can only have negative effects on them in the long term, I have been actively involved in passing this knowledge along to young parents through articles, interviews, lectures, booklets, and my Web site. Occasionally I address high school students in the hope of conveying this critical information to them before they marry and have children of their own. Although in many of these encounters I sense an ingrained reluctance to face this topic, I also have the frequent impression of touching a chord in these teenagers, of raising an issue that has long been waiting to be addressed. Wounds cannot heal as long as they are covered up and denied.

What has surprised me about these adolescents is that initially they hardly appear to know what I am talking

about. They look at me as if I have come from some other
planet and say things like, "I've never heard that before."
"Yes," I reply, "it's probably rare for someone my age to be
speaking this way." "No," they rejoin, "it has nothing to do
with age. Everyone says you can't raise children without
hitting them from time to time. There were those cranks
like the hippies and the parents in the sixties who wouldn't
lay a finger on their children. But they weren't raising
them—they were just neglecting them. Now that their
children have grown up, they all complain about the lack
of discipline, the absence of anyone telling them what to
do and what values to live up to. You only have to look
around to see what becomes of children who haven't been
brought up strictly enough. They're left to do exactly as
they like, then they start playing around with guns, and in
the end they run amok and kill their schoolmates. That
kind of thing doesn't only happen in America. You get it in
Europe as well."

These young people are identifying closely with the
opinions of their parents. But the minds of adolescents still
going through a process of emotional and intellectual up-
heaval are not yet completely closed, and I repeatedly find
that despite their protestations I am getting through to
them. Many of them are prepared to entertain the argument that teenagers who attack schoolmates do so not because their doting or indifferent parents have allowed
them to behave exactly as they liked, but because they have

been seriously neglected and maltreated and have had no chance to react to that treatment other than by accepting it. The rage pent up inside them is like a time bomb that detonates as destructive hatred. When I explain this to students, I can tell from their faces that they know precisely what I mean. Their bodies are still very close to that knowledge and, unlike adults, they do not yet say, "Yes, but despite those beatings I have grown big and strong. And ultimately it's my parents' cuffs and blows I have to thank for it." Their memories of being beaten go back not fifty or sixty years but less than ten.

One seventeen-year-old whose parents were both teachers had this to say: "My parents love me and they did everything right. At first they never hit me, but later they had no choice. As a child, I got up to all kinds of nonsense. I was always doing something stupid." The boy made a very intelligent impression, but he was also quite restless and anxious. I asked him if he could give an example of what he meant by "nonsense." "Well," he said, "when I was ten I ran away from home, and it took my parents six hours to find me. Of course they gave me a hiding, and today I'm convinced they were right to punish me. I never did it again, I can tell you! I got up to other kinds of nonsense instead. It's the way I am. I was probably just born bad." I probed further. "Have you ever asked yourself why you do things like that? Why did you let your mother look for you for six hours? Were you trying to hurt her? Try and

feel your way back into the ten-year-old you once were."
The boy did not look at me, but from his face I could see
that a change was going on in him. His studied arrogance
was rapidly disintegrating. After a while he said, "I remember thinking as they hit me that if they spent all that
time looking for me so desperately, they must love me after all. Their anger is a proof of their love." "Well," I said,
"if you ran away to test their love for you, you can't call
that nonsense. Maybe you had no other proof of their affection." "Yes, I suppose that's one way of looking at it. I
always had the feeling I was a burden for my parents, that
they'd be glad if I didn't exist. But their anger showed me
that it wasn't true." "So, that ten-year-old boy acted intel-
ligently and systematically. Why do you call that nonsense?" "I don't know. I just thought I was a naughty boy."

Here we have an instance of the way a person can spend
a whole childhood wearing the label "I'm bad, stupid, a
nuisance, a burden" and never challenging that view because it appears to be shared by those in his immediate environment. Parents attach such tags as an expression of the
things they find hard to take from their children. And the
things they find hardest to take are those that are likely to
awaken their own traumatic memories. But children need
not remain the prisoners of such labels. All that is needed
is a teacher able and willing to help them to question their
validity. My experience with school groups suggests that
this is not so difficult, but it is certainly rare.

I visited a group of young mothers at two-month intervals. At the first meeting I distributed a booklet I had written on the detrimental effects of slapping infants as well as
older children. I asked the young mothers in attendance
with their babies whether this was a problem for them.
One woman said that, of course, she would slap her baby to
show her what she wasn't allowed to do. But she did it quite
dispassionately, she felt. Another said that she sometimes
slapped her baby inadvertently. A third said her little boy
was fond of crumbling cookies over the carpet. Her slaps to
teach him that this wasn't allowed had not done the trick,
and her own mother had told her that the child went on
doing it because she wasn't strict enough with him. I asked
if it was the desire to teach her son good manners that
made her slap him. Suddenly she broke down and said,
"No, I'm always so sorry for him. But I have to do the right
thing. Everyone in my family says I'm spoiling him and
bringing him up to be a tyrant. What can I do?" I asked the
young woman whether she had been beaten as a child. "Of
course," she said, "it's the only way I know."

At the second meeting I posed the same question to the
woman who "dispassionately" disciplined her baby. She responded that when she was little she had frequently been
beaten by her parents with belts and coat hangers, and
they had always made it clear how furious they were with
her. She, however, punished her baby without any emo-

tional involvement. She didn't want her little boy to suffer from her anger, for she loved him, but she could not understand why he was so timid and clinging. I asked her if she could imagine that he might be afraid of the next beating he was in for. "Oh no," she said, "he is too small to think so." She believed in all sincerity that although the child was too small to be afraid, he was sensible enough to understand the objectives she was pursuing by spanking him. She had no idea that the only thing a child can be taught that way is to be afraid.

Returning to the group for the third meeting, I was astounded by the process that had been set in motion among these women. They were beginning to see their children not as objects to be whipped into shape but as persons whose eyes, tears, and behavior were sending messages to which these mothers had suddenly developed a receptivity. Probably the intimacy established between the child and the nursing mother had helped them to face up to the challenge in the questions I had asked them; the close union with their children meant that they no longer felt so alone. That same closeness had also released their own infant needs from the bonds that had kept them hidden away for so long. Their bodies had remembered with heightened intensity the frustrations they had suffered in early childhood and the wall of ignorance and unfeeling cruelty they had been up against.

One of the women told me she had recently learned from her sister that when she was two years old her mother had bitten her and drawn blood. This took place in a family where together the parents had established a reign of violence. During our first meeting this woman had been all but impervious to the subjects I was raising. Guided by her intellect rather than her emotions, she said she was undergoing a course of neurolinguistic programming that would help her avoid repeating that pattern. But at the second meeting she broke down in tears and told the group of her suffering and her desperate attempts to be a different kind of mother to her child than her own mother had been to her. The courage she displayed in breaking free of the tradition she had grown up with was astounding. When she related the episode of the two-year-old child being bitten, a number of women broke down and wept. They could hardly bear to listen because they were being assailed by their own memories. They expressed their astonishment that one could love a mother capable of such cruelty, but at the same time they discovered in themselves a potential for cruelty of which they had been completely unaware until then. The women were unanimous that the work in the group was helping them to keep that potential under better control, as they now understood where it came from and thus no longer felt helpless and in its thrall.

In her book *Le Pardon Originel* the Swiss theologian Lytta Basset writes that we cannot eradicate evil because we are doomed to repeat the things that have already happened. All we can do is accept the presence of evil and pardon others and ourselves so that we can achieve as much freedom as possible. She agrees with me that we must recognize what has been done to us in order to be able to forgive. The difference is that for me the emphasis lies not in the act of pardon but in the possibility of taking childhood reality seriously instead of denying it.

As a therapist I know that we can free ourselves from inherited patterns if we can find someone to believe us and stand by us, someone who instead of moralizing wants to help us live with the truth. My personal experience and my experience with clients have shown me that there are indeed ways of freeing ourselves from evil that are not dreamt of in the philosophies of the theologians.

Sincerely forgiving our parents (not just because some code of morals tells us we ought to) is not difficult once we have allowed ourselves to feel the distress they caused us, to take it seriously, and to fathom the full extent of their cruelty. A woman is fully able to imagine that a nice person cruelly treated in childhood might be capable of cruelty as an adult. A woman experiencing that urge in her own behavior toward her child, and being as honest with herself as the mothers in that group, can certainly relate to that possibility. In time she will be capable of forgiveness. Yet it is not forgiveness that will liberate young mothers but understanding that they are not alone with their knowledge, that they no longer have to deny the truth, that they are in a position to recognize evil for what it is. This kind of security can be achieved in such groups.

The compassion of the others for the woman so cruelly mistreated as a baby was so direct and sincere that this woman felt empowered to rebel against her parents for the first time. She told me later that from then on, her feelings for her children changed drastically. She no longer saw them as little things doing their utmost to distress her but as helpless creatures for whom she was prepared to accept responsibility. And she was able to do so because the child she once was had started to grow. Before then that child had been locked away in a cell with its fear of parental violence.

Many of us leave that child within ourselves in its prison, in constant fear, isolated from the knowledge that could set it free. Once that child has shaken off its chains, been allowed to see and to judge what it sees, it can walk out of its prison on its own. The fear is gone because it has recognized the manipulations for what they are. It is not afraid to see because it is not reduced to silence, because it can say what it sees, because it is not alone with what it has seen but has its perceptions confirmed by an enlightened witness. That witness has at last given the child what its parents withheld: the confirmation that its perceptions are right, that cruelty and manipulation are precisely that and nothing else, that the child need no longer deceive itself into seeing them as a form of loving care, that this knowledge is necessary in order for the child to be genuine and capable of love, and that the fruit from the tree of knowledge is there to be eaten.

For the first time these young mothers are able to feel something that is quite normal for a loved and sheltered child to feel: oneness with themselves. They can trust their senses, they need no longer actively conspire in their own deception, and they can at last feel at home in their own inner selves. They are no longer fugitives and can now allow themselves their own true feelings, trusting quite rightly that those feelings will tell them nothing other than what belongs to themselves and their histories. It is not surprising, then, that some of them begin to question the ideology of La Leche League. They discover that it was their own wish to nurse their first child until the age of five and that the child had adapted to the wish of the mother. With the second child the mother could fully respect the child's need for autonomy.

In the chapter "Sandra and Anika" of my book *Paths of Life* I describe conversations between adult women and their elderly parents. Do such exchanges have a therapeutic effect? My view is that if the parents are ready and willing to listen and to express their feelings openly, such encounters can have therapeutic benefit for both them and their grown children. But if the parents persist in maintaining that they know best, there will be no foundation for any genuine exchange. In the two examples in *Paths of Life* both daughters had been through extended courses of therapy, which enabled them to frame their questions in such a way as to obtain responses that would truly help them. They managed to break through their parents' defenses and at the same time keep a watchful eye on their own emotions.

What helped these women to speak calmly and not to give vent to emotions that would have thwarted the dialogue was not a therapeutic attitude. We cannot practice therapy on our parents when we need something from them. These two women were in quest of more information and thus did not have the freedom therapists have in engaging with a client's emotions. Sandra and Anika, though adults, also stood as children in seeking a genuine dialogue with their parents. That is the essential difference between their concerns and those of a therapist.

How were these women able to keep their tempers when their parents showed the same lack of understanding they had displayed to them as little girls? In therapy Sandra and Anika had learned to accept the strength of their emotions and to take them seriously. They thus gained control over those feelings and no longer could be bullied by them into acting them out against their own interests. They now had the freedom to experience and decide which feelings they wanted to show to whom. If they had been through a form of therapy that remained at the cognitive level without reaching their feelings, they would probably have been in danger of losing control in the confrontation with their parents or else clamming up, and then no real exchange could have come about.

Do parents have to have been through therapy in order to be equal to such an exchange? That would, of course, be ideal. An intense conversation with adult children who have achieved awareness is a big challenge for elderly people and confronts them with feelings they have long repressed. When they sense that they can no longer blame their children for what has been done to them, repressed emotions from their own early childhoods may surface. Therapy that could give them the chance to work on those emotions with someone else (this is possible at any age) might indeed have helped them understand themselves better.

But therapy is not indispensable for such an exchange. The main thing, I believe, is the attitude adopted by the elderly parents. Even without therapy they can take what their children have to tell them as an occasion to reflect on their earlier lives and ask themselves what kind of an impression they made on their children as young parents. But that can only be possible when mothers and fathers no longer unconsciously assume that their children have been brought into the world to alleviate the frustrations and repair the damage they have suffered in their own lives.

Adult children can also confuse childhood reality with present reality. This confusion may express itself in the way they treat their own children but comes across just as clearly in the way they act toward their parents. I once knew a forty-year-old woman who was unable to find a partner or a satisfying job and persisted in placing the blame on her mother. She accused her of not having had enough time for her when she was small and of not protecting her from her incestuous father. The mother, herself an incest victim, had indeed failed to see what was going on under her own roof.

The elderly woman was so appalled by the incest that she was prepared to go to any lengths to atone. She apologized constantly for her earlier failings and accepted all the blame her daughter heaped on her, even when it had to do with things over which she could have had no possible influence. The daughter, unable or unwilling to give up the image of her beloved father, used her mother as a scapegoat. She remained caught up in this attachment to her mother instead of assuming responsibility for her feelings and actions like a grown woman.

Meanwhile her mother remained caught up in her own childhood reality, living in constant fear of the next punishment from her own mother and ready at all times to confess her guilt. In this symbolic context her daughter turned into the strict, vengeful mother whom she hoped to placate by being "good" and from whom she hoped to receive forgiveness. Her pleas for some sign of love and reconciliation aggravated her daughter's feelings of powerlessness. Naturally, no genuine love could grow from such an attachment. What took shape instead was a bond of hatred that deepened the self-deceptions of both women. The daughter hoped to avoid engaging with her image of her father by using the mother as the target for her anger. The mother chose not to see that her daughter was not her mother, and that she had a right to a life of her own that should not be thwarted by the mother's guilt feelings.

Exchanges between the generations can be very helpful if both sides have the courage to open their hearts, listen to each other, and not hide behind a wall of silence or power. This mother-daughter relationship, however, was far from achieving anything constructive. The daughter exploited her mother's readiness to do penance so as not to have to take responsibility for her own life; the mother exploited her daughter by making her into her own mother, cowering from the task of showing her her limits and defending herself against unjust accusations. She feared both her own feelings of anger and revenge and those of her daughter. If someday they manage to accept and freely express their feelings, they might penetrate to the sources of those feelings in both their lives. The frankness of such a dialogue would allow both sides to grow; they would be astonished to realize that their anxieties had lessened, that they had regained their original capacity to love and communicate freely.

9

WITHOUT

ENLIGHTENED

WITNESSES

---

*T*HE SINCERITY and courage displayed by the
young mothers I described in the last chapter cast
light on something that has to my knowledge yet to be il-
luminated by the psychoanalytic community: the difficulty
of a mother who was herself abused as a child. However
well her defenses may have masked her feelings about her
past, they may well break down at the birth of her first
child unless someone is on hand to support her in bringing
that past reality into full awareness.

In detailed examples in my book *Thou Shalt Not Be
Aware* I showed that psychoanalysis has failed to address
this phenomenon. Idealization of the mother runs through

the whole history of psychoanalysis, which even in its more recent modifications has elected to concentrate on the structures of the child psyche. The Kleinian school, drawing from the work of Melanie Klein, has its roots in the attempt to spare the mother and place the blame on the child. Although Donald W. Winnicott got closer to the reality of the mother, he too remained ultimately trapped in idealization. To illustrate my contention, in this chapter I offer as an example the life story of the psychoanalyst Harry Guntrip, based on Guntrip's own account (published in 1975) of the two analyses he himself underwent and on Jeremy Hazell's 1996 biography of Guntrip.

Harry Guntrip suffered most of his life from severe physical symptoms and total amnesia in connection with the death of his younger brother, Percy. He desired nothing more fervently than to fill in the blanks of his own childhood, of which he could remember only that his mother often struck him violently, usually on the mouth. When he had grown up, she told him that she had never wanted to have children and had breast-fed him for an extended period of time only in order to avoid getting pregnant again. She also told him that she had once bought herself a dog but soon had to part company with it because of the irresistible temptation to whip it every day.

Guntrip's mother was the eldest of eleven children, whom she had to look after on her own because her mother, a celebrated beauty, had no interest in their development and no time to give them the care they needed. After the childhood she had been through, it is hardly surprising that the last thing Guntrip's mother should have wanted (as she freely admitted) was to have to take care of another set of small children, a task that had been beyond her powers the first time around. She wanted freedom, travel, and recognition of herself as a person. Not surprisingly, she did not look forward to Harry's birth and was unable to love him when he came into the world.

In 1930 a general practitioner diagnosed Harry, who was then a young man in his late twenties, as suffering from severe sinusitis. When the condition did not respond to medication, Guntrip underwent a radical operation that removed all his front teeth as well as the surrounding bone and periosteum. This left his mouth without an anchor for dentures, so that from then on he was uncomfortable eating in the company of others and avoided doing so. Worse still, the operation failed to end the severe bouts of sinusitis he suffered every winter.

Guntrip spent more than a thousand hours undergoing psychoanalysis with Ronald Fairbairn, whom he admired and was grateful to for spending so much time with him. But as he himself reports, the sessions did him little good. Fairbairn interpreted Guntrip's "preoccupation with the bad mother" between his third and fifth years of life as

"sexualized relations with a castrating mother in the oedi-
pal phase." (Although Fairbairn ventured to question
Freud's drive theory, he appears to have retained his allegiance to its concepts in his practice.) After this long and
unavailing ordeal, Guntrip approached Donald Winnicott
for help. and, as it turned out, received much more warmth
and empathy from him than he had from Fairbairn. In
"only" 150 hours of sessions, until Winnicott's death in
1971, Guntrip was able to recognize much more clearly the
extent to which he had been rejected by his mother, but this
did nothing to remedy the amnesia surrounding his
brother's death. Shortly after Winnicott's death Guntrip
discovered he had cancer, which was already in an advanced
stage. In January 1975 he underwent a last-ditch operation,
but it was unsuccessful, and he died the following month.

Both Guntrip's and Hazell's accounts indicate that
Guntrip adopted Winnicott's interpretation that his mother
had loved him in his first few months of his life. Winnicott
was firmly convinced that she had rejected the child because external circumstances had proved too much for her.
Guntrip made a brave attempt to integrate the "good" and
"bad" objects in the way his analysts suggested, but his
body could not be deceived. It knew that his mother had not
loved her firstborn child from the outset. Because of her
own repressed history, she had been unable to love him.

For an outsider such a truth is relatively easy to accept,
but for the child in question it is inconceivable. And it will

remain inaccessible to the adult analysand unless he is given the help he needs to confront and sustain this knowledge.

Guntrip wanted to believe what Winnicott told him. He clung to this illusion with all his might, and I am convinced that the price he paid for it was the disease that killed him. The night after Winnicott's death Guntrip dreamed about his tragic relationship with his mother. In that dream she was not even aware of the existence of her baby and remained engulfed by depression. In the next two weeks there followed a series of dreams that revealed the whole truth to him and helped him overcome his amnesia. Here is his description of the last of those dreams. "In the dream I saw a brightly-lit room with Percy in it. I knew it was him. He was sitting on the lap of a woman with no face, no arms and no breasts. She was only a lap to sit on, not a person. He looked very dejected and the corners of his mouth stayed down-turned when I tried to make him laugh." My opinion is that the Percy in the dream was also a representation of Guntrip himself. The amnesia disappeared once there was no analyst there to keep the truth away from him. But Winnicott's affectionate empathy with his situation as a child helped Guntrip finally admit the truth to himself in his dream.

In Guntrip's view, this sequence of dreams was the harvest of twenty years of analytic work. But now he was alone with the truth, a truth that contradicted everything Winnicott had upheld. What he needed at this moment was the presence of an enlightened witness. Alone he could not face the truth: his mother, on her own admission, had not wanted him *from the outset*—in other words, when he was still in the womb. Winnicott was concerned to spare Guntrip the truth, either out of fidelity to his own theories or because he himself had inhibitions about entertaining the idea of a mother who cannot love her own child.

This incapacity to love from the outset occurs much more often than we imagine. It is not the fault of the mothers but of the ignorance of society. In a progressive maternity ward a woman having her first baby should have access to enlightened assistance in perceiving and becoming fully aware of the body memories surfacing within her. This would prevent her from passing on the traumas of her own childhood (abandonment, violence, and so on) to her baby.

What right do I have to criticize Winnicott's interpretations? Is it not presumptuous for an outsider to talk about the limitations of a specific course of psychoanalysis, knowing many fewer details of the case than the two persons involved, the analyst and analysand, do? I do not think it is presumptuous. We have not only the right but indeed the duty to query the limitations of illustrious figures in the history of psychoanalysis (or any other field). They did not have the information that we do and from which we can profit today. In the light of what I have learned over the past forty years about the dynamics of child abuse and its denial, I feel confident in asserting that Winnicott's interpretations were not only demonstrably in conflict with the truth but also confirmed the analysand in his self-delusions and thus worked against his recovery.

If Guntrip's mother had had the emotional potential (afforded by a happy childhood or the awareness of her suffering as a child) to love her firstborn child, her attachment to him after birth would have occasioned a profound intimacy. It would then have been impossible for her thoroughly and radically to negate the very existence of that child. *The Scientification of Love*, Michael Odent's book on the "love hormone," explains the mechanics of this process impressively. Rejection of a firstborn child is exclusively the consequence of the mother's repressing, and hence remaining unaware of, her own personal history. This repression can inhibit the release of this all-important hormone.

If such a mother encounters people who are able to help her break through to her own childhood and bear its truth, she will be free to love her child. I see this happen again and again in groups such as I have described in the previous chapter. Women having their first child can fully develop the capacity to love it if they have the support of people trained to provide the proper assistance, people who themselves know about the consequences of early cruelty. In order to train enough people to supply such help, professionals must stop camouflaging what we should know today with theories and idealizations of yesterday.

10

THE

HEALING POWER

OF TRUTH

I SOMETIMES GET letters from people who find my books convincing and are grateful for the information they contain but who find it hard to bear the consequences of this knowledge. They torment themselves with feelings of guilt. Many of them are aware that those feelings have their roots in childhood, when they were blamed and punished whenever something went wrong. But they cannot free themselves of the pain it causes them to realize they were unable to give their own children what they needed because of how they themselves were treated in childhood. Most of these letter writers are women who had their first children in the 1950s and 1960s. At that time it was common practice in maternity wards to separate mothers from their newborns, for little was known about the emotional needs of infants.

We all know mothers and fathers of that generation who insist that their parenting methods were right. They are determined not to be shaken in their conviction that what they experienced at the hands of their own parents was just and proper. We also know elderly people who go on treating their adult children with little or no respect, demanding affection and attention from them as if they had a God-given right to receive their care, respect, and love regardless of how they treated their children when they were small. Such parents frequently persist in trying to dominate their adult children with all the means at their command so as to demonstrate the power they still have over them.

Some of the older women who write to me, however, are prepared to engage in a real encounter with their adult children and want to do their best to find an empathic response to their children's criticisms of their parenting style.

It is never easy to admit one's errors. Like so much else, this is an ability we should acquire in childhood but can also develop in later in life. If instead of punishment for our errors we received a loving explanation of what was wrong or dangerous about what we had done, we are able to respond with spontaneous regret and integrate the realization that to err is human. But if we were always punished by our parents for the slightest offense, then we integrated a very different kind of knowledge: that owning up to our mistakes is dangerous because it loses us the affection of our parents. The legacy from this experience can be permanent feelings of guilt.

A woman told by her grown daughter that the beatings she gave her have damaged her for life can respond in a variety of ways. She can say, "I'm sorry, but I was beaten when I was little, and as a mother I thought I had to do the same. I'm grateful that you've told me how much it made you suffer. I never knew that. It now helps me to understand your behavior as a child. I ask you to forgive me. It was ignorance that made me act as I did." Or she can say: "Your friend Annette was beaten and she never had any problems later on. It's obviously not so important what parents do or don't do. Perhaps it's genetic."

In the latter case it is unlikely that the daughter will feel inclined to carry on the conversation. In the former, much will depend how the daughter has developed in adulthood. She may be satisfied with the mother's response and proceed from there to build a new and trusting relationship with her. But there may be reasons why she cannot do that and will instead continue to heap reproaches on her mother's head and keep repeating how much she suffered from the power her mother exerted over her. If this kind of pattern establishes itself, the mother can always attempt to escape those reproaches by saying, "At my age I cannot go on listening to your criticisms because they hurt me too much. You're a grown-up now, and you have to take your life in your own hands. I do not feel it is fair of you to blame me for the things you do and the decisions you make." But a mother can adopt this attitude only if in her youth she was not subjected to extreme corporal punishment and was allowed to make mistakes. There are also many mothers who were punished for every little thing by their own parents and perpetually blame themselves or allow themselves to be blamed. They behave like small children trying to be good so as to earn the love of their parents and not to be alone.

The cardiologist Dean Ornish emphasizes the significance of emotional attachments in the lives of elderly heart patients and demonstrates that those who do not survive their illness have frequently been suffering from loneliness and isolation, while those who have maintained close family ties have better chances of recovery. This may seem plausible, but I have found that many patients cling to the very attachments that have played a strong causative role in their illness. Some of them manage to free themselves from their illness if they have the good fortune to encounter enlightened witnesses who help them dig down and find their own personal truth.

This can happen at any age, as the following story illustrates. It was sent to me by a reader after the death of her friend, then seventy years old, whom I will call Katya.

Katya was born in the north of France and was the oldest of three girls. Her mother, strict and self-righteous, demanded of her eldest daughter unconditional submission and a standard of performance at school well in advance of her years. This she achieved with the aid of a martinet—a short whip consisting of several straps attached to a wooden handle, produced in France for use on animals but often used by parents to punish their children. Katya was expected to be the best in her class, and whenever she came home with anything less than top grades she was beaten for her "sins." Though an excellent student, she lived in constant fear of her mother's scathing reproaches. Her mother suffered frequent migraines and other painful conditions, all of which she blamed on her eldest daughter. Katya was constantly attempting to find a way to relieve her mother's suffering.

It was Katya's job to look after her two sisters. Whenever they failed to live up to their mother's standards, Katya was punished for it. The parallels to the tale of Cinderella are obvious. My experience over the last few decades has taught me that the dynamics in that fairy tale occur more frequently than we might expect in real life.

How was Katya able to develop her above-average intelligence? How did she contrive to satisfy her mother's demands, at least to the extent of being able to survive and not turn to crime later in life? Who was the helping witness in Katya's life? Her father? Hardly. He was a weak person who had abused Katya sexually; he died of lung cancer when she was twelve.

For a long time Katya was unable to remember any adult from whom she had received anything besides correction and cruelty. But once, when she was about fifty, she happened to meet a former playmate from her old neighborhood who told Katya, "I loved and admired you so. Can you remember your maid, Nicole, who was so affectionate to you and spoiled you when your mother was away? When your mother was there, Nicole was afraid of her." Katya was very surprised. She had no memory of this maid who must have played an important part in her life because, despite the abuse she heard and received from her mother, Katya had grown into a lovable and strong person. No one else in her childhood supported her and showed respect and affection for the person she was.

As an adult, Katya was good at her job, but her private life was a succession of mishaps. She loved a man who abused her trust and then ended up marrying someone she did not love. She had wanted children but could not love her son as she would have wished. Intent on being different from her own mother in every possible way, she never beat the child, but she was incapable of protecting him from his cruel father. From the outset her relationship to her son, born a year after her marriage, was marked by the experiences she had been through. She had no knowledge of what a child feels because she had never permitted herself to feel how she had suffered as a small child at the hands of her mother. As her own feelings were alien to her, she was unable to relate to her son's feelings. Her understanding of him was fatally flawed by this lack of knowledge about herself. From the very beginning the main feelings she had for him were pity and guilt. She sensed how unhappy he was, but she was powerless to do anything about it.

Thus she repeated her own fate in her relationship with her son. Like her mother, she wanted to do everything right, but she lacked the knowledge that comes from a good attachment between a young child and a caregiver. In her own life, including her marriage and her relationship with her son, she was dogged by guilt. Just as she had been blamed for every misfortune that befell her mother, father, and sisters, she blamed herself for the suffering of her husband and son. Her husband was adept at exploiting her attitude to delegate to her the feelings he had split off from himself—helplessness, anxiety, powerlessness—and thus avoid living with them himself.

Katya was like a sponge: she absorbed all those feelings without realizing that it was not in her power to work out other people's feelings for them. Only her husband could have understood and come to terms with his own emotions. But instead of refusing to take over the feelings he cast upon her, she accepted them without protest because emotionally she was still the little girl who felt responsible for her parents' suffering. It took a long time for her to admit that she had married a man who strongly resembled her mother, a man without the slightest interest in thinking about his own behavior and profoundly incapable of relating to others. For twenty years she hoped that with kindness and understanding she might be able to change things for the better, but the nicer and kinder she was to him, the more aggressive he became, because above all he envied her for her kindness. This she only recognized much later. After years spent soliciting her husband's affection, she developed severe internal bleeding. Her uterus was removed, and she sought psychotherapeutic help.

Even then Katya remained blind to the fact that as an adult she had ways of escaping her dilemma, that she could have separated from her husband. Instead, she sought ways of living with him without incurring outbursts of anger. She asked a psychoanalyst what she could do to live in peace with her husband: the very sight of her appeared to provoke a towering rage in him, so there must be something wrong with her. The analyst said she could not help her become the kind of person who could live in peace with her husband; she could only help her to be the woman she was and to find the courage to live with the truth.

Katya felt that her analyst understood her dilemma, but at the same time she feared the idea of separating from her husband. Her feelings of guilt prevented her from setting herself free.

Why was her therapist unable to help her understand that her husband's behavior had its roots in his childhood and his hatred of his mother? If she had truly achieved adulthood Katya could certainly have understood that, but within herself she was still the child who took all the blame for the bad moods and the failures of the people around her. And this made her all but incapable of seizing the opportunity offered to her. She wanted to leave her husband to save her own life; her body had unmistakably shown her how imperative this was. Yet she was unable to take that step. The child within her lived in fear, and that fear was reinforced by her husband's threats that he would kill himself if she left him or even so much as mentioned separating. But thanks to the therapist's decisive support, Katya finally did manage to go through with a separation.

Katya went to live alone. She made new friends and had a job she enjoyed. She felt relieved to have escaped the misery she had been living in, but the shadows of childhood caught up with her in her relationship with her son. He suffered from his parents' separation and then divorce but, like his father, was unable to show his true feelings. Having been beaten and humiliated by his father and misunderstood by his mother, he had developed into a suspicious person. He could not believe that anyone could like him as he really was, and was always trying to be stronger and more powerful than anyone else. He had experienced his father as a merciless judge, and now he played that role with his mother, blaming her for all the problems and disappointments he had failed to come to terms with in his own life. Katya was fated for this role, for she had been programmed in childhood to provide the ideal scapegoat.

She lived in hope of one day being able to talk it out with her son, to hear him tell her what he had suffered, to understand him, to tell about her own feelings and find some common ground. This hope lived on in her for decades, although all the circumstances indicated it could never be fulfilled. Her son shied away from any heart-to-heart exchange with her, but he never told her why. She tried to find an explanation for his behavior, doing everything in her power to reach out to him and stubbornly ignoring the pain this caused her. She explained his emotional inapproachability as resulting from the fact that when he was small she had been unable to give him the unconditional love he so badly needed. Her compassion for him was limitless, but in the process of sympathizing with him she gradually lost touch with her own feelings. Sometimes, when she could no longer avoid confronting the hatred she thought she sensed in him, she wept bitterly. Her illusions were a product of her own need; it was the pain she felt that confronted her with the truth. At one point she asked her son, "Why do you hate me?" His response was indignant. He told her she must be confusing him with his father and did not see him as he really was. Katya thought this quite likely and blamed herself for projecting her earlier experi-

ences with her husband onto her son. She did not dare confess to herself that she genuinely did not know what he was
like, so she persisted in talking herself out of her true feelings and clinging to her illusions.

As she had learned as a child from her own mother, the
adult Katya forced herself every day to believe what she was
told and not to see what she saw. Although this compulsion
was a source of immense suffering, she was unable to rid
herself of it and desperately sought a solution, yet she still
refused to perceive the roots of her troubles in the relationship with her mother. She convinced herself that she could
live with her son's refusal to engage in genuine communication with her. But she was deceiving herself. Her longing for
understanding was stronger than her good intentions.

By means of another serious illness her body succeeded
in rousing her from her delusions. Only then did she realize that she was gradually killing herself with her submissive attitude toward her son. She was forced to realize, just
as she had twenty-five years before with her husband, that
all her attempts to understand her son were futile as long
as he refused to open himself up to her, and that her desire
to empathize with his reproaches could not be fulfilled as
long as he refused to trust her. But such trust was entirely
beyond him because the foundations for it had never been
established in his early childhood.

Katya's unfulfilled desire for an emotional and intellectual exchange with her parents, sisters, and schoolmates

had survived for so long in this illusory form, and was now so exclusively directed at her son, that she was unable to see how strongly he rejected that desire, and that he had good reasons to actively fear it. Nor was she able to respect his fear. She was intent on paying the debt of guilt she had incurred as a mother, and if there was no other way, she would do it by suffering.

What did she feel guilty about? That as a mother she had not been able to stand by her child when he needed it most, that during his birth she had allowed herself to be intimidated by the nurses, that she could not trust her feelings, that she had sometimes left him in the care of others because she thought they must be better at caring for him than she was? Surely, her friends told her, one cannot give something one has never had. Was she such a perfectionist that after fifty years she was still unable to forgive herself for her mistakes? It looked very much that way. But why had she become such a perfectionist, why could she not forgive herself for her failings? It was up to her to put an end to this game. Why could she not bring herself to do so?

To confront these questions seriously, Katya had to face up to her earliest childhood, when her mother used physical force to make her a good girl deeply ashamed of everything she did wrong and living in a state of constant guilt. The lessons she learned retained their impact throughout her life. Katya's potential for guilt was almost unlimited.

Many educators preach the use of physical correction from the outset to teach children obedience. These methods, they say, are all the more effective the earlier they are put to use. Katya's life story confirms those theories. True, she was able to develop her creativity and establish relationships. In her work as a vocational guidance counselor she was even able to help others. But all her life she was incapable of ridding herself of the guilt her mother had implanted in her at such an early age. The seed thus sown grew into a tall tree and effectively obscured a view of the facts.

Giving up such an attitude at an advanced age is anything but easy. But it is not impossible. Katya finally succeeded in drawing the right conclusions from her insights and abandoned her illusions. There followed a long struggle with herself and a harrowing mourning process. But her body told her in no uncertain terms that this was long overdue and the only way she could save herself.

All her life Katya had submitted herself to well-established guidelines. She had accepted all kinds of laws that played a major role in dictating her behavior. These were, in the first instance, the injunctions of the Catholic church with which she had grown up. Now, at last, she questioned the code of morals her parents had lived by. She combed the libraries in search of writings by theologians speaking out unequivocally against the physical correction, humiliation, neglect, and manipulation of children. Apart from the seventeenth-century churchman John Amos Comenius—a Protestant—she found no one upholding such opinions. The suffering of children was simply not on the theological agenda. And in the psychological literature she increasingly turned to, the central message was that one could regain one's health only by having positive feelings and thoughts because negative emotions like anger and rage were toxic to the body.

So all this searching in books was to no avail, and it could not have been otherwise. It is true that feelings of impotent rage can act on the body like a poison, but as long as its sources are unknown or ignored there is no way of ridding oneself of it. The feelings of hatred resulting from the helplessness of a little girl trying to communicate with her parents but invariably rebuffed are only too understandable. As long as Katya insisted on regarding her son's criticisms and accusations as justified and blaming herself for the deprivations he suffered in childhood, she was bound to remain caught in a trap from which there was no escape.

Once Katya was able to abandon her childhood hopes, to feel clearly her needs and to look for their fulfillment in a realistic way, her hatred disappeared, because she had granted herself the freedom to accept the facts of her present and past realities. She no longer had to force herself to believe in things for which she could see no justification, to adopt the viewpoints of others and to burden herself with them. She no longer had to force herself to overlook facts and deny her perceptions, because now she was allowing herself to entertain the thoughts that welled up in her and to feel the feelings that were appropriate to her situation.

These are the changes that enable us to overcome hatred. Hatred can survive only as long as we feel trapped in the situation of a child who has no choice, who is forced to hold out in hopeless circumstances in order to survive. As soon as the adult sees an alternative, a way out of the trap, the hatred disappears of its own accord. It is then entirely unnecessary to preach morality, forgiveness, or exercises in positive feeling.

The idea that we can arouse positive feelings in ourselves by engaging in relaxation training or meditation is one that I feel to be profoundly illusory. But again and again I come across advice of this kind, coupled with the assurance that one will free oneself of one's symptoms by forgiving one's parents and substituting positive feelings for negative ones.

I know of no one who has actually achieved this in the long term, but many authors unflaggingly counsel forgiveness as a form of therapy. If their various recommendations do help, so much the better. But they did not help Katya. In her story I find confirmation of my conviction, born of decades of experience with clients, that in the long run feelings cannot be manipulated. If we suppress them, feelings can indeed hide themselves from the conscious mind, but they frequently resurface in the form of bodily symptoms, which conceal their real content and intensity, making it much more difficult to deal with them than it would be if they were admitted to consciousness.

When our anxieties make us afraid, we may try to distract ourselves for a while by, say, going out for a good meal. But our body may not be able to digest it. Then the meal becomes not a source of nourishment but a burden of which the body frees itself by a bout of vomiting or diarrhea. A process like this does nothing to get rid of the original anxiety; it merely masks the sources of it even more effectively than before. Such processes can leave traces on the body in the form of various maladies ranging from slight to extremely severe.

When Katya fell seriously ill, the rebel in her awoke and she was able to tell herself: Even the worst criminal can stop blaming herself when she has atoned for her crimes. Katya was no criminal; she was a mother like many others in this day and age, a mother who had not learned how to welcome and cherish her newborn baby, whose body had never stored any positive messages from her own mother.

On several occasions Katya had apologized to her son for her failings and expressed sorrow for the things she had done wrong. Now it was time to rid herself of the guilt feelings that were poisoning not only her life but also her relationship with her son. She had finally to accept that what has happened in the past cannot be undone, and that despite all her efforts she had not succeeded in gaining her son's trust, just as he had not succeeded in trusting his mother. There was no way that he could repair the damage done to their past; it was a task completely beyond his means. The path he chose—shutting himself off—was perhaps the only way of putting together a life for himself and avoiding damage from his mother's projections.

The account Katya's friend sent me included no details on Katya's son. Here I am dependent on the information the friend received from Katya and which of course is colored by Katya's experiences as a mother. My assumption is that when she stopped looking to him to act as a stand-in for her father and mother and was able to face squarely the full reality of her childhood, he was able to break loose from her and no longer felt the constant urge to use her as a target for his accusations and criticisms.

In her childhood no one understood Katya, not even her little sisters, who needed her as a mother. Later, at boarding school, though she did make friends with one girl who took an interest in her, Katya was already so marked by her experiences with her mother that she had become suspicious and unapproachable and was unable to grasp the opportunity to develop warm friendships. As an adult she longed for close relationships but invariably chose partners unable to fulfill that desire, men who were afraid of emotional closeness. When her son grew up, she felt she finally had the right to demand an open and frank response. Her son may well have sensed this implicit demand when he was small without being able to put a name to it, and it may have caused him such suffering that he needed to dodge the emotional intensity of the demand. In his mother he sensed the needy child to whom he was unable to relate.

Ultimately Katya resigned herself to the fact that the tragedy of her childhood had deprived her of any chance to be a better mother. Once she had learned to accept her fate, she was able to enjoy the final stages of her life in tranquillity. She had satisfying relationships with her friends, made peace with herself, and no longer set herself unrealistic goals.

In therapy Katya realized how much her relationship with her son had been burdened by the shadows of her childhood, and memories of her mother came back to her more and more clearly, memories of the way she had refused to relate to her eldest daughter. Katya was now able to feel her infant needs and express them in a diary, from which her friend sent me an excerpt after Katya's death:

As your child I had a right to your love and affection but I had to abandon those rights. The child had nowhere she could go and say: I'm hungry, give me something to eat; I don't understand the world, explain it to me; I'm afraid, stand by me; I feel sorrow, comfort me; I'm helpless, help me; I feel exploited, stand up for me; I'm breaking apart, I feel so small in the face of all the things I cannot do, take those burdens from me; I need someone with eyes for my distress, look at your little girl, look at me! Today I understand all this but as a child I did not feel those needs. All I did, and did unceasingly, was to try to please you by being good at things, and that went on throughout my life. Now I don't need to please anyone, only to be true to myself. I want to understand my fate, accept it and stop burdening my own son with it. Suddenly there are people who understand me. I don't need to fight to get them to do it. They are there. Perhaps they were always there but I was not free enough to see them.

Her friend added the following note:

I wanted to confront you with Katya's story because at first I thought it was an exception, somehow at odds with the things you have written in your books, things I consider to be correct. This story didn't seem to fit because it showed the opposite case so clearly, a mother suffering in her relationship with her adult son and not as in all your other cases the sufferings of children at the hands of their parents. But when I read Katya's therapy notes after her death, I understood that the roots of this mother-son conflict lay much deeper down. The effects of Katya's unhappy childhood were probably already very strong before her son was born and they pursued her all her life. From this perspective he had very little chance of devel-

oping what was within him as long as he remained in her
proximity. He needed that emotional withdrawal from
her. Tragic as it may seem, it was probably the only
chance he had to save his life from the insatiable emotional expectations of his mother.

I'm not blaming Katya for this. I loved her dearly and
in her efforts to be genuine and true she was always an
example to me. But only now, after her death, do I see
that all her attempts to understand her child, to do him
justice, while at the same time remaining true to herself
were doomed to fail, doomed by the history of her own
childhood. Whatever she tried, fate gave her no chance of
living openly and trustingly with the person nearest to
her without giving up her own truth, because she had no
ideal to emulate, no one in her original family had been
accessible for the kind of communication she was looking for. By later projecting her expectations onto her son
she contributed actively—albeit unintentionally and unconsciously—to giving this relationship the tragic absence of warmth and closeness that she had suffered so
badly from as a child.

I used to think that's the way life is, you can't choose
your own destiny. But now I think that if you're allowed
to make your own choices as a child, if you're allowed to
develop in accordance with your gifts instead of constantly having to live up to your parents' ideals, then you
won't end up choosing a partner where you're not free to

say what you want to say. The conclusion is unavoidable: a kind of behavior we may once have thought completely irrational can in fact reveal itself to us as the logical consequence of real events which will, however, usually remain hidden.

I'm glad that Katya left me her notes. They have helped me understand a great many things in my own life.

Katya's story illustrates how the deprivations of childhood can deceive an intelligent adult into looking exclusively to her child for the gratification of her profoundest needs. And it also shows that by becoming able to take those needs seriously, thanks to the assistance of an enlightened witness, a person can give up even very old projections and finally find peace.

FROM
IGNORANCE
TO KNOWLEDGE
AND COMPASSION

---

*I*N *ANGELA'S ASHES* Frank McCourt graphically describes the trouble a child was likely to get into as recently as the 1960s by asking questions adults preferred not to answer. Little Frank soon realized that in many cases the adults were at a loss for an answer but couldn't afford to admit it. Either they took refuge in cryptic allusions ("You'll understand that when you're older. Now go out and play") or they simply told him to shut his mouth and go about his business.

Today things have changed. It is less dangerous to have an independent and inquiring mind. We can no longer tell children to go out and play, leaving them alone with their questions. Older children have almost unlimited access to information via the Internet, which gives them a whole new kind of independence from their parents.

As a child I, too, had to learn to keep my mouth shut and to stop asking "Why?" of people whom I knew would give me an evasive answer. Later I tried to answer those questions for myself and in so doing discovered the supreme commandment running through our upbringing and education: "Thou shalt not be mindful of the things done to you or the things you have done to others." I then realized that for thousands of years this commandment has prevented us from telling good from evil, identifying the wrongs done to us in childhood and sparing our own children the same fate. In all my books I have tried to point out that the causes and effects of cruelty to children are identical: if we deny the wounds inflicted on us, we will inflict those same wounds on the next generation. Unless, that is, we make a decision in favor of knowledge.

Sooner or later it will become firmly anchored in the public mind that if we beat our sons and daughters we are doing them harm and not displaying our love for them, and that we no longer have the right to delegate our responsibility to the apostle Paul. By persisting on that course we are creating the very evil we are trying to beat out of our children. Corporal punishment generates fear, frequently inducing in a child a state of stupor in which mental reflection is completely ousted from the child's con-sciousness by panic. Many people growing up in the tradi-tion of poisonous pedagogy appear to remain in such a stu-por all their lives, in permanent fear of new blows. As my discussion of Stalin in Chapter 6 showed, new experiences and information have no impact on fears deposited and stored in the child's body at an early age, and no impact on the barriers in the mind resulting from them. In certain cases the blows children receive will prevent them from achieving genuine adulthood and accepting responsibility for their own words and actions. And so they remain emo-tionally crippled throughout their lives, tormented chil-dren unable to recognize evil for what it is, let alone to do anything about it.

Like Frank McCourt, many people today say, "My child-hood was awful, but it had its moments, and the main thing is that I survived it all and can write about it. It's the way of the world." I find such an attitude fatalistic and be-lieve that we can rebel against this kind of childhood and do our bit to ensure that it will cease to exist, or at least cease to be so common.

To a child, an unemployed father (like McCourt's) spending his dole money on drink is an inescapable trick of fate; the child has no alternative but to come to terms with such realities. Children may in some vague way intuit that they are not really being perceived by their parents for what they are, that the parents need them as scapegoats.

But their minds cannot grasp the fact. A child's body may register that it is being starved of affection, but children have no hope of explaining to themselves why things are as they are. They take refuge in compassion for their parents, and the feeling of love will help them retain some modicum of dignity in spite of the mistreatment.

But children forced to overlook the cruelty born of irresponsibility and indifference on the part of their parents are in danger of blindly adopting this attitude themselves and staying bogged down in the fatalistic ideology that declares evil to be the way of the world. As adults they will retain the perspective of the helpless child with no alternative but to come to terms with its fate. They will not know that, paradoxically, they can only grow out of this childlike attitude if they lose the fear of the wrath of God (their parents) and are willing to inform themselves about the destructive consequences of repressed childhood traumas. But if they do become alive to this truth, they will regain their lost sensibility for the suffering of children and free themselves of their emotional blindness.

The figure of Jesus confounds all those principles of poisonous pedagogy still upheld by the christian churches, notably the use of punishment to make children obedient and the emotional blindness such treatment inevitably brings. Long before his birth Jesus received the greatest reverence, love, and protection from his parents, and it was in this initial and all-important experience that his rich emotional life, his thinking, and his ethics were rooted. His earthly parents saw themselves as his servants, and it would never have occurred to them to lay a finger on him. Did that make him selfish, arrogant, covetous, high-handed, or conceited? Quite the contrary.

Jesus grew into a strong, aware, empathic, and wise person able to experience and sustain strong emotions without being engulfed by them. He could see through insincerity and mendacity and he had the courage to expose them for what they were. Yet to my knowledge no representative of the church has ever admitted the patent connection between the character of Jesus and the way he was brought up. Would it not make eminent sense to encourage believers to follow the example of Mary and Joseph and regard their children as the children of God (which in a sense they are) rather than treating them as their own personal property? The image of God entertained by children who have received *love* is a mirror of their very first experiences. Their God will understand, encourage, explain, pass on knowledge, and be tolerant of mistakes. He will never punish them for their curiosity, suffocate their creativity, seduce them, give them incomprehensible commands, or strike fear into their hearts. Jesus, who in Joseph had just such a father, preached precisely those virtues.

But the men of the church, themselves deprived of a happy childhood, could only pay lip service to those values. As the Crusades and the Spanish Inquisition show only too clearly, they acted in accordance with what they had been through in childhood, and those acts were destructive, intolerant, evil in the profoundest sense of the word.

Even those who sincerely champion the cause of goodness are often inclined to defend the system in which they have grown up, still thinking that the blows they received were necessary and beneficial. The fact that not one theologian (with the exception of Comenius) has ever spoken out against physical "correction" for children shows that this practice has long been part of the childhood experience. Two thousand years after Christ, we can in fact say that his teachings have yet to find their way into the church.

In time, the gulf between these two opposing value systems will narrow because the members of the upcoming generations will have the courage to call evil by its name. In isolated cases we can observe this already. At a conference in February 2000 Germany's minister of justice, Herta Däubler-Gmelin, was heard to say, "That old homily about loving parents being obliged to 'beat some sense into their children' is dangerous balderdash. Violence is learned in the home and passed on from there. We have to explode this vicious circle." Whoever first propagated the kind of thinking Däubler-Gmelin was attacking was without doubt a product of the traumatic style of upbringing I call poisonous pedagogy. It is high time to relinquish the destructive models and to mistrust the principle of obedience. We have no need of docile children brainwashed by

their upbringing to be ideal targets of seduction by terror-
ists and lunatic ideologists, ready to fall in with their commands even to the extent of killing others. Children given
the respect they deserve from their earliest years will go
through life with open eyes and ears, prepared to fight injustice, stupidity, and ignorance with arguments and constructive action. Jesus did this at the age of twelve, and the
scene in the temple (Luke 2:41–52) demonstrates elo-
quently that, if need be, he could refuse the obedience his
parents asked of him without hurting their feelings.

With the best will in the world we cannot truly emulate
the example of Jesus. None of us were carried by our mothers as the child of God; indeed, for far too many parents,
children are merely a burden. What we can do, provided we
really want to, is learn from the attitude displayed by
Joseph and Mary. They did not demand docility from their
son, and they felt no urge to inflict violence on him. Only if
we fear the confrontation with our own histories will we
need to have power over others and cling to it with all our
might. And if we do that it is because we feel too weak to
be true to ourselves and our own feelings. But being honest
to our children will make us strong. In order to tell the
truth we do not need to have power over others. Power is
something we only need in order to spread lies and
hypocrisy, to mouth empty words and pretend they are true.

If the insights of well-informed experts (like Frédéric
Leboyer, Michel Odent, Bessel van der Kolk, and many

others) were to reach a large number of parents, and if those parents had the support of religious authorities in following the example of Mary and Joseph, it is entirely realistic to imagine that the world would be a much more peaceful, honest, and rational place than it is today.

The stricture "Thou shalt not know the difference between good and evil" was in place before the Ten Commandments. According to Judeo-Christian tradition, it stood at the very beginning of human history. But it is destructive rather than constructive. The aim of this book has been to point that out in no uncertain terms. Today we stand poised between the primeval commandment of ignorance and the abundance of information we now have on the destructive effect of emotional blindness, of insensitivity to the suffering of children. We can draw on this information to spare our children and grandchildren the unnecessary suffering and evil our ancestors grew up with. Doing precisely that is, to my mind, a debt we owe to future generations.

Today we know how much good can develop in children who are not forced to grow up in fear of their parents. These children will be immune to the teachings of those biblical authors representing the father as a jealous God, unpredictable and unjust, even downright cruel. They will refuse to accept his ascriptions of guilt and will enjoy the pleasures of discovery. Buoyed by the experience of genuine love and affection in their childhood, they will unerringly identify the injustice of the Creation story and take advantage of the current opportunities for communication (Internet, television, travel) to disseminate what they know. In so doing they will arouse the curiosity of others and support them in the joy of discovery and new knowledge. In this millennium, Adam and Eve can free themselves of the guilt caused by their so-called sins and finally become truly adult human beings.

BIBLIOGRAPHY

Basset, Lytta. *Le pardon originel*. Geneva: Labor et Fides, 1995.

Bowlby, John. "Violence in the Family as a Disorder of the Attachment and Caregiving Systems." *American Journal of Psychoanalysis*, vol. 44, no. 1 (1984): 9–27.

Busnel, Marie-Claire, et al. *Le langage des bébés: Savons-nous l'entendre?* Paris: Jacques Grancher, 1993.

Capps, Donald. *The Child's Song: The Religious Abuse of Children*. Louisville, Ky.: Westminster/John Knox Press, 1995.

Carrère, Emmanuel. *L'Adversaire*. Paris: P.O.L., 2000.

Goleman, Daniel. *Emotional Intelligence*. New York: Bantam, 1995.

Guntrip, Harry: "My Experience of Analysis with Fairbairn and Winnicott. (How Complete a Result Does Psychoanalytic Therapy Achieve?)." *International Journal of Psychoanalysis*, vol. 56, no. 5 (1975): 145–156.

Hazell, Jeremy. *H. J. S. Guntrip: A Psychoanalytical Biography*. New York: Free Association, 1996.

Hirigoyen, Marie-France. *Stalking the Soul: Emotional Abuse and the Erosion of Identity*. New York: Helen Marx Books, 2000.

Karr-Morse, Robin, and Meredith S. Wiley. *Ghosts from the Nursery: Tracing the Roots of Violence*. New York: Atlantic Monthly Press, 1997.

Kershaw, Ian. *Hitler, 1889–1936: Hubris*. London: Penguin, 1998.

Leboyer, Frederick. *Birth Without Violence*. Rochester, Vt.: Inner Traditions, 1995.

LeDoux, Joseph. *The Emotional Brain*. New York: Touchstone, 1996.

Luhrmann, T. M. *Of Two Minds: The Growing Disorder in American Psychiatry*. New York: Knopf, 2000.

Maurel, Olivier. *La Fessée: 100 questions-réponses sur les châtiments corporels et l'éducation sans violence*. Paris: La Plage, 2001.

McCourt, Frank. *Angela's Ashes*. New York: Touchstone, 1999.

Miller, Alice. *Banished Knowledge*. New York: Anchor/Doubleday, 1991.

_____. *Breaking Down the Wall of Silence*. New York: Meridian, 1997.

_____. *The Drama of the Gifted Child*. Revised edition. New York: Basic Books, 1996.

_____. *For Your Own Good*. New York: Farrar, Straus and Giroux, 1996.

_____. The Forbidden Issue. Web site, http://www.alice-miller.com.

_____. *Paths of Life*. New York: Pantheon, 1998.

_____. *Thou Shalt Not Be Aware*. New York: Farrar, Straus and Giroux, 1998.

_____. *The Untouched Key*. New York: Anchor/Doubleday, 1990.

Niehoff, Debra. *The Biology of Violence: How Understanding the Brain, Behavior, and Environment Can Break the Vicious Circle of Aggression*. New York: Free Press, 1999.

Odent, Michel. *The Scientification of Love*. London: Free Association, 1999.

Ornish, Dean. *Love and Survival*. New York: Harper Perennial, 1999.

Pennebaker, James W. *Opening Up*. New York: Guilford Press, 1997.

Pert, Candace B. *Molecules of Emotion*. London: Simon & Schuster, 1998.

Project NoSpank. Ed. Jordan Riak. Internet Web site, http://www.nospank.org.

Rosenbaum, Ron. *Explaining Hitler.* New York: Random House, 1998.

Sapolsky, Robert M. *Why Zebras Don't Get Ulcers.* New York: Freeman, 1994.

Schacter, Daniel L. *Searching for Memory.* New York: Basic Books, 1996.

Shapiro, Francine. *EMDR: The Breakthrough Therapy for Overcoming Anxiety, Stress, and Trauma.* New York: Basic Books, 1997.

_____. *Eye Movement Desensitization and Reprocessing: Basic Principles, Protocols and Procedures.* New York: Guilford Press and Mark Peterson, 1995.

Stern, Daniel. *Diary of a Baby.* New York: Basic Books, 1992.

_____. *The Interpersonal World of the Infant.* New York: Basic Books, 2000.

Van der Kolk, Bessel. *Psychological Trauma.* Washington, D.C.: American Psychiatric Press, 1987.

Waite, Robert G. L. *The Psychopathic God: Adolf Hitler.* New York: Basic Books, 1977.

Zimmer, Katharina. *Erste Gefühle: Das frühe Band zwischen Kind und Eltern.* Munich: Kösel, 1998.

_____. *Gefühle: Unser erster Verstand.* Munich: Diana, 1999.

ACKNOWLEDGMENTS

WHEN I STARTED to work on this book, I asked many parents, young and old, rich and poor, from farmers to professors, how they felt about corporal punishment. To my dismay, the vast majority of them felt that spanking was an important part of child discipline, that indeed one cannot raise a child successfully without it. So I worried about the reception of this book, because it takes such a strong stand against that practice. Who will agree with what I have to say, I wondered? Will editors and publishers be open to its message?

But I needn't have worried. Indeed, I found in Winfried Hoerning at Suhrkamp an editor who has been thoroughly engaged in my work, and who has brought to *The Truth*

Will Set Your Free both his professional expertise and his own experience as a young father of three children. I also appreciate the professional and human qualities of my editor at Basic Books, Jo Ann Miller, who edited *The Drama of the Gifted Child* and has been familiar with my ideas since then. These enlightened and friendly midwives have been of invaluable assistance in bringing this book into the world.

I want to thank the many people who told me their stories and allowed me to use their letters, personal conversations, and transcripts from group workshops. I learned a lot from all of them. I extend my gratitude as well to Olivier Maurel, who, while working on his own book about corporal punishment, shared with me his research on educational practices around the world. His observations and conclusions offer ample confirmation of what I have learned from my therapeutic experience. Finally, I am grateful to Jordan Riak, executive director of Parents and Teachers Against Violence in Education, for the important information I found on his Web site, www.nospank.org, and for his ongoing personal support and encouragement.

ABOUT THE AUTHOR

ALICE MILLER has achieved worldwide recognition for her work on the causes and effects of childhood traumas. Her books include *The Drama of the Gifted Child*, *Banished Knowledge*, *Breaking Down the Wall of Silence*, *Thou Shalt Not Be Aware*, and *For Your Own Good*. Miller maintains a Web site (www.alice-miller.com) and corresponds with readers from all over the world, many of whom credit her with freeing them from the shackles of their childhood suffering. In 1986, Alice Miller was awarded the Janusz Korczak Literary Award by the Anti-Defamation League. She lives in Switzerland.